Contents

Hutchinson Checkbook Series

Comprehension

Bill Deller and Mike Taylor

Series Editor

NOTTINGHAMSHIRE EDUCATION DEPARTMENT,
THE FRANK WHELDON COMPREHENSIVE SCHOOL,
ENGLISH DEPARTMENT.

Other titles in the series

Punctuation Philip Payne
Spelling Martin Tucker
Summary Ken Methold and Roy Blatchford
Literature Roger Lewis, Martin Pugmire and Gill Pugmire
Writing Linda Cookson
Oral Roy Blatchford and Melvyn Elphee

Hutchinson & Co. (Publishers) Ltd

An imprint of the Hutchinson Publishing Group

17–21 Conway Street, London W1P 6JD

Hutchinson Group (Australia) Pty Ltd
16–22 Church Street, Hawthorn, Melbourne, Victoria 3122

Hutchinson Group (NZ) Ltd
32–34 View Road, PO Box 40–086, Glenfield, Auckland 10

Hutchinson Group (SA) (Pty) Ltd
PO Box 337, Bergvlei 2012, South Africa

First published 1985

Set in 10/12 Century Schoolbook
by Oxprint Ltd, Oxford

Printed and bound by Anchor Brendon Limited, Tiptree, Essex

British Library Cataloguing in Publication Data
Deller, Bill
Comprehension.
1. English language—Examinations,
questions, etc
I. Title II. Taylor, Mike
428.2 PE1114
ISBN 0 09 149291 2

Introduction: You and the text

It is easy to think that when we are reading our eyes are simply lifting someone else's words or ideas off the page rather like a powerful magnet.

This is only partly true.

Often we can only make real sense out of what we are reading by becoming equal partners in building up the meaning.

For instance, if a friend passes us a scrawled-on piece of paper, we naturally have a go at guessing the meaning of it even if a few words are 'unreadable'. Similarly, part of the fun of reading a good story is the way we use what we already know about people and events to guess what might happen next. A poem about loneliness or boredom will only have real meaning for us if it triggers off vivid memories of times when we ourselves were lonely or bored. Our own experience fills out the meaning. At other times we may get angry about something we are reading because we don't agree with it or because it contains misleading mistakes. We feel we know better than the writer.

Reading is, then, more than a mechanical activity. It is more like talking to someone. Readers bring the words on the page to life – by making use of their interests, by comparing the message with what they already know, by asking questions, by guessing what might be coming next, by getting angry, happy or even confused–just as in everyday conversation.

This is what comprehension is all about.

We hope that the readings we have collected together in this *Checkbook* are interesting and varied, and that the tasks we have suggested will help you to become a more active and effective reader.

Talking through these activities with others will provide a more useful and enjoyable way of improving your reading and getting to know your strengths and weaknesses as a reader than just writing the answers. For this reason we suggest that many of the tasks are best done in pairs or small groups.

The activities in this book may not always look like the comprehension exercises set for tests and examinations. However, since they encourage you to be more active, thoughtful and selective in your reading they will help you to improve your examination techniques as well.

If some of these activities help you to think about your reading and to try out different ways of reading for different purposes, then this is far more important than whether your answers are 'right' or 'wrong'.

Many of the conclusions you arrive at will probably be different from those of other students. This is as it should be, since it shows that you are an active reader. Your individual experiences and attitudes have helped to bring the text to life.

In the end though, the only sure way of becoming a good reader is not to work your way solidly through this or any other comprehension book. What you must do is to get into the habit of reading as much as you can. Pick books you like reading and as you read more and more, you are likely to get better and better at it.

1 What's missing?

Information

When we are listening to someone interesting, we become 'tuned in' to what they are saying. Our brains not only follow their pattern of thought, but think ahead, preparing the ground for what might be said next. Similarly, in a noisy high street, we may not 'hear' every word said in a conversation, but our brains fill in any interruption with sensible guesses so that we do not lose the sense.

The same is true of reading. Guessing what might be coming next is a part of building up the meaning and thinking alongside the writer on the page.

The following activities draw attention to this important aspect of reading, and will help you to improve it.

A Lifesaving

Over the page are some instructions for lifesaving. Unfortunately, some of the words have been scratched away by vandals. However, it is still quite possible to understand most of the instructions by putting sensible words in the gaps.

➔

- Read through the lifesaving instructions a sentence at a time and make a list of all the words which would make sense in each of the gaps. You might find it easier and more interesting to do this with a partner.

  For some gaps you will probably come up with several sensible possibilities.

- Always read to the end of the sentence before deciding which word or words might make sense. Some of the clues which can help you may occur later in the passage after the gap.

- Once you have made your list, read the instructions right through again and decide which version sounds best, and makes the most complete sense.
- Then check your version with the original.

LIFESAVING

If someone is drowning, keep [redacted] and quickly decide which of the following life-saving [redacted] will be most [redacted] in the circumstances.

1 If the victim is near the [redacted], lie down on the bank and [redacted] out a hand to him. If he is [redacted] of reach, find a pole, [redacted], or some other suitable [redacted] which can be held out to him.

2 If the victim is some [redacted] from the bank, [redacted] him a rope or [redacted] that will float to give him [redacted] and give the rescuer [redacted] to think about what to do [redacted].

3 Wading is usually [redacted] than swimming, and if [redacted] wade out carrying a pole or branch which can be [redacted] out to the [redacted] and then used to pull him into [redacted] water

4 If the [redacted] is a long way from the bank, [redacted] a boat is quicker than [redacted] but only if the [redacted] is able to row.

5 If none of the [redacted] methods is possible, [redacted] out to the victim and [redacted] him back to safety. Remove shoes and outer [redacted] if possible as these will [redacted] progress through the water. Always walk [redacted] into the water if the [redacted] is unknown.

Answers on page 99

- Now discuss these questions:

1 How did you manage to 'read' words which weren't even there?
2 What different clues did you make use of?
3 Would this skill be useful on other occasions? For instance, reading hard words or reading in a foreign language?

B Lost in the jungle

This is part of an imaginary story, in which the intrepid American aviator, Amy Waterson, is lost in her light aircraft *Dora* over the Amazon jungle. Years later, a zoological expedition comes across some burnt-out wreckage in a small jungle clearing. Among the wreckage are some badly charred and weatherbeaten remains of Amy's log book.

- Can you read the last page? Using the same method as before, discuss what the missing words might be and write down your agreed list.
- Try to work out what happened during Amy's last days from this evidence.

C Poem

Here is a poem about an old, retired man. At this stage, the author is uncertain about some of the words and has left them out.

- Read the poem carefully then put in words which seem to fit the general mood or description.
- Compare these with a partner by reading both versions of the poem and discussing which one you prefer.

When he was eighty-two they opened
the first of the Supermarkets
on the main road. I don't think
he even noticed the mighty ———
of tins and washing-up liquid
at cut prices ——— in the window
although one Sunday morning
he caught in bare hands
the panful of boiling peas
that ——— from his black hob.

The house was ——— and dirty;
it stank as if death were there already:
you couldn't be sure in rooms
where you ——— as though through water
that hadn't been changed for years.
Of course, you never stayed long (the stench,
the dinginess, the look that showed —
again – he didn't know who you were),
but let him for his pride's sake brew
a pot of tea, and ——— for awhile
among his ——— memories, which,
towards the end came down to one.

It was ——— to visit him by then:
to step from the main road's redevelopment,
the loaded shopping-bags, the lines
of ——— cars, into that hush
where over and over he lifted arms
like trembling ———, pulled the trigger,
and killed it for the Duke – the last
stag on the great estate
that has been a public park for fifty years.

Now that you have produced your own version of the poem there is only one piece still missing – the title. Often the title of a poem is like a key which helps to unlock its meaning.

- Invent a title which will help another reader to understand what this particular poem is about. Lastly you might like to compare your versions with what the poet himself wrote.

Answers on page 99

D Short story

Here is the framework for a complete short story. Most of the details are missing, however.

- Read through the outline first, to get an idea of the shape of the whole story.
- Then have a go at writing your own story by filling the gaps with ideas of your own. You need only fill the early gaps with a word or phrase, but later gaps need to be completed with a phrase, sentence or several sentences.
- When you have finished, read through your version of the story and make sure that it is interesting and that it makes sense.
- Then compare what you have written with a partner, and decide which version you like best.
- Last of all, invent a suitable title for the story.

My name is ________________ and I go to ________________ school.

The story I am going to tell you is a very ________________ one. It all happened after school on a ______ night, as I was going ________________ from school.

As I went out of the school gates I was feeling ________________ because ____ .

I was just crossing ________________ road, when out of the corner of my eye I saw ________________. At first I couldn't believe what I was seeing, so I ________________ nearer. To my complete surprise ________________.

I had to decide what to do quickly so I ________________________________ ________________________________.

Things moved quickly after that and I will try to tell you exactly what happened. ____ ____ ____ .

While this was going on I was feeling ________________ and I wondered if ________________________.

At last I managed to say something.

'____,' I said.

'____,' was the reply.

Just then I caught a glimpse of a ________ some distance away and I ______ ____ .

At last I managed ______ ________ and ____ .

Finally I got home, opened the door and saw my mum in the kitchen, making a cup of tea. 'What's been happening to you today, then?' she asked, looking up.

'____,' I replied.

E Readers' letters

The following are answers to readers' letters sent to different teenage magazines.

- Read the answers carefully, finding all the clues which tell you about the reader's original enquiry.

One way of doing this is to make notes of any words or details in the magazine's reply which would help you to answer these questions.

–Who is the letter writer? How old is he or she?
–How many other people seem to be involved? Who are they?
–What seems to be the writer's problem?
–What exactly do they seem to be asking for advice about?

Re-reading the replies with these questions in mind and talking over the points with a partner will help you to find all the clues.

- Now use your notes to write your own version of the missing letter.
- After you have written it, read it with the answer and see if the two together make sense.
- Compare your versions with other people's and decide which is best.

a)

No, you'll have to tell them the truth and face up to the anger and disappointment they will feel. It was a very stupid thing to do, as you have broken their trust and it will take a long time to build it up again. They thought you were responsible enough to be left at home while they were away for their fortnight's holiday and you have proved them wrong.

Since the damage can't be paid for through insurance, then I suggest you make some contribution towards the cost. You must also apologize profoundly to your parents and promise never to do such a foolish thing again. The fact that they keep the car parked in the street is no reason for trying to lie your way out of the situation you have got yourself into.

b)

Moving to a different school in a different and unfamiliar area is a very unsettling experience, not least of all because the voices around you don't sound like the ones you are used to.

People can be very cool towards those they don't know and I think this is more likely to be the cause of the problems you are now facing than the way you speak.

The best thing you can do is act naturally and be yourself. Gradually everything will fall into place, and remember it can take time to build up good friendships. I'm sure that people are not making fun of you behind your back as often as you are imagining.

Your accent is often heard on radio and television nowadays, and lots of superstars in the sporting and pop worlds share it with you.

So give up trying to be someone you aren't, because you'll never get on with people if you put on an act.

c)

The best policy is to ignore them, because sooner or later they're going to get bored with taunting you, especially if you won't give them any money. And on no account give in to their demands. It was a silly thing to give them money in the first place. The way they were spending it couldn't have done their health any good since we are all aware of the dangers of smoking nowadays. Also, if your mum finds out that you haven't been eating at lunch times, as she thought, your own health could be in danger as well! However, if these two older girls do get nasty and carry out their threats, then you must get help. You may not think it's nice to run telling tales, but you must tell someone for your own good, such as an older brother, sister or your parents.

Answers on page 100

2 Fitting it together

Information

A piece of writing usually has some sort of order or logical sequence to it. A good reader will pick up, even without knowing it, the clues that connect what she or he has just read with what is coming next. As we read, our minds are busy making links between the pieces of information we are given. We store up essential facts and ideas as we go along, ready to compare them with what is coming next. Paragraphs are often used to split up a text into manageable chunks, each paragraph containing an idea, a stage in the argument or a part of the story and each one having connections with what comes before and after it.

All the following passages have been jumbled up so that the paragraphs (or in the case of the poem, the verses) are in the wrong order. You have to use your skill as a reader to put them in the right sequence so that the passage or poem makes sense.

A Passport to peril

The following seven paragraphs describe the war-time exploits of Odette Sansom who worked for the British in Nazi-occupied France during the Second World War. They are printed in the wrong order.

→

- Read them through and then try to put them in the correct sequence.
- First of all decide which section *sounds* like either a beginning or an end. Beginnings often set up or describe a scene. They may also provide background information, or act as an introduction, tempting the reader to read more. Endings often have a sense of completeness, and may start with 'signal' words like *lastly* or *in conclusion*.

- To fit together the paragraphs in-between, look for other 'signal' words like *next, also* or *however*. Also, try to decide where in the passage a character, theme or other detail is first mentioned, since it is likely to be referred back to several times in the whole passage.
- When you have fitted the paragraphs together, compare your version with a partner, and discuss any differences you might have. Then look up the original order on page 100.

PASSPORT TO PERIL

a Odette proved a first-rate member of the team, but she came under suspicion. One day a German officer, Lieutenant Bleicher, approached her, having convinced one of her colleagues that he carried peace proposals between anti-Nazi Germans and the British and Americans. Could he get in touch with London? Odette was suspicious. Playing for time, she drew up plans for the team's dispersal. Peter Churchill was away at this tense moment and when he returned he was even more suspicious than Odette had been. They must escape.

b Finally, her captors sent her to Ravensbrück concentration camp. Sometimes her female guards treated her well enough, sometimes savagely, but Odette miraculously survived her ordeal until final victory. A heroine of the war, she was awarded the greastest of non-military honours, the George Cross.

c It turned out that British Intelligence was interested in more than her photographs. At an interview she was asked if she was prepared to work in her beloved homeland, alongside the French Resistance Movement, in the struggle against the Nazis. Despite the very real risk to her life, and despite having three young children, Odette agreed. In October 1942, she landed in the south of France, becoming the radio operator of another British agent, Peter Churchill, who had been in that country since January.

d Too late! They were both seized by the Gestapo. After several weeks in a number of local prisons, they managed to speak to each other briefly when being taken to yet another one, and they agreed that they should claim to be husband and wife. After some torture Churchill was sent to a concentration camp in Germany, where he survived until the war's end.

e When Odette Sansom, the French-born wife of a Briton, took some holiday snaps in Boulogne, she never dreamed that they would involve her in a series of dangerous adventures which would bring her close to death–more than once . . . .

f In the summer of 1940, when most of the British army had been safely brought back from Dunkirk, they left behind them a Europe which was now virtually in the hands of Nazi Germany. Plans to stop the Nazis taking over completely began at once. The War Office put out a request for photographs of the French Channel coast. One of those who replied was Odette. She sent in some snaps of Boulogne, which is situated in an area which she knew very well

g Odette was treated even more harshly. Bravely, to take the heat off Churchill, she claimed to be leader of the group. She endured no less than fourteen grim interrogations and was tortured time and time again. Some of her toenails were torn out and the base of her spine was branded with a red-hot iron. But nothing would make her talk.

- Now answer these questions:

a) How did Odette first make contact with the War Office?
b) What particular qualities did she have which led the War Office to ask her to be an agent?
c) After their capture, what did Odette do to help keep Churchill alive?
d) What do these words or phrases mean in the passage:
   (i) plans for the team's dispersal
   (ii) survived her ordeal
   (iii) grim interrogations
e) Where do you think this version of Odette's story came from?
   –From a book by Churchill about the French resistance?
   –From a history textbook?
   –From a magazine for young people?
   –From an encyclopaedia?
   What clues helped you to answer this question?
f) Do you like the title of the story? Give reasons why you think it is or it isn't appropriate. Then make up another title for it yourself.

Answers on page 100

B The lesson

The next piece of writing is a poem. It describes one teacher's answer to unruly classes! Each verse tells a part of the story.

- Read all ten verses and then put them in the order that you think makes the best sense.
- Use the same sorts of clues that you found helpful in the last activity. Do you think there is more than one possible order?
- Compare your version with a partner's and discuss any difference you have. Then compare your versions with the order on page 101.

THE LESSON

A poem that raises the question:
Should there be capital punishment in schools?

a 'Please may I leave the room sir?'
a trembling vandal enquired
'Of course you may' said teacher
put the gun to his temple and fired.

b Chaos ruled OK in the classroom
as bravely the teacher walked in
the nooligans ignored him
his voice was lost in the din.

c The teacher surveyed the carnage
the dying and the dead
He waggled a finger severely
'Now let that be a lesson' he said.

d 'The theme for today is violence
and homework will be set
I'm going to teach you a lesson
one that you'll never forget'

e The first blast cleared the backrow
(where those who skive hang out)
they collapsed like rubber dinghies
when the plug's pulled out.

f And when the ammo was well spent
with blood on every chair
Silence shuffled forward
with its hands up in the air.

g He picked on a boy who was shouting
and throttled him then and there
then garotted the girl behind him
(the one with grotty hair).

h He threw the sword at a latecomer
it struck with deadly aim
then pulling out a shotgun
he continued with his game.

i The Head popped a head round the doorway
to see why a din was being made
nodded understandingly
then tossed in a grenade

j Then sword in hand he hacked his way
between the chattering rows
'First come, first severed' he declared
'fingers, feet, or toes.'

- Now answer these questions:
  a) What is capital punishment?
  b) Who do you think the 'nooligans' are? Why is this a good word to describe them?
  c) Why is the line 'first come, first severed' funny?
  d) Following the same kind of rhyme and rhythm as the original, write an extra verse of your own, and decide where it would best fit in the poem.

Answers on page 101

C Making cheese straws

The following passage is a set of instructions for making cheese straws. Under the *Method* heading you will find a list of twelve instructions. They are in the wrong order. Your task is to arrange them in such a way as to enable someone to make cheese straws successfully.

In this example you will have to draw a lot more upon *your own* experience of cooking.

➔

- Read carefully through the list of utensils and ingredients and start to build up your own idea as to the likely order of events. For instance, will you cut the mixture *before* or *after* grating the cheese? Will you roll the mixture *before* or *after* adding the egg?
- Once you have thought through the possible order of events, go through the muddled instructions and put them into a logical sequence.

CHEESE STRAWS

Before starting you must have the following utensils and ingredients

UTENSILS

mixing bowl	small bowl
sieve	flour dredger
knife	grater
tablespoon	rolling pin
teaspoon	baking tray
fork	cutters
	serving dish

INGREDIENTS

180 g (6 oz) flour	80 g (3 oz) margarine
¼ teaspoonful salt	80 g (3 oz) cheese
pinch cayenne pepper	1 egg or egg yolk
pinch mustard	a little water

METHOD

a Place on the greased baking tray.
b Grate cheese and add to the mixture.
c Flour table and knead mixture until smooth.
d Preheat oven at 180°C (350°F) or gas mark 4 and grease a baking tray before you begin.
e Sieve flour, salt, pepper and mustard into a bowl.
f Turn mixture over and roll out thinly.
g Bake for about 15 minutes on a middle shelf of the oven until a straw colour.
h Remove from baking tray, cool and serve.
i Rub in margarine until it resembles fine breadcrumbs.
j Beat egg and add this also.
k Mix all these ingredients to a stiff paste and add a little water if necessary.
l Cut into 0.5 cm (¼ in) wide fingers.

Answers on page 101

D The gates

The extract on page 24 comes from the first chapter of a story.

Everything is the same as in the original *except* that the paragraphs have been jumbled up. It is quite difficult to put the paragraphs back in the right order, so you will have to use every clue you can.

- First, read the paragraphs through, to get a rough idea of what the story might be about.
- Then, answer these questions. This will help you to decide on the order of the paragraphs.

  a) Who is the central character of the story?
  b) Where is the story set?
  c) What does the character feel about being there?
  d) What strange experience does the character have?
  e) What does he or she decide to do about it?

- Now decide which is the opening paragraph and which might be the last. Then fit the others together in the order which makes the best sense. It is much easier to do this with a partner or group.

Answers on page 101

THE GATES

a Once outside the school gates he stopped to think. He buried his face in his hands and, in the darkness they made, he could think clearly.

b Geoffrey Moller approached the gates of Elgan Comprehensive School. He hated those gates. He hated everything to do with school. How he dreaded those mornings when he sat nervously on the corner of his bed and literally shook with fear, for he knew that if he kept on playing truant, he would be taken 'into care'.

c Geoff took his hands away from his eyes, ran up to the bus stop and sat on the wall opposite it, shaking. The bus came, and Geoff got on and sat upstairs on the top deck. There was nobody except him. He felt a bit better as he closed his eyes and breathed in relief as well as air.

d 'It's just a dream, 'he thought. 'Yes, I'm not here at all. I'm at home in bed.'

e Geoff had been attending Elgan, on and off, for about a year. During that time he had been experiencing attacks of dizziness. The first time Geoff could remember undergoing the dizziness, was when he was standing in the playground, watching some boys playing football. All of a sudden everything was like a dream. He had never felt so strange in all his life. Geoff knew he was in the playground, but it just didn't seem like it. It was as if he was watching someone else on a film. He closed his eyes, then opened them again, but it was still the same. He felt as if he was in a trance.

f 'I've got to get home', he thought desperately. 'Number 47 bus at the top of the road. It'll take me right home.'

g Then, he suddenly came out of the trance and realized that he really was in school. The reality hit his mind like a ton of bricks. He panicked and ran to the school gates. He had to scramble over them in order to try and get home, which was the only place he wanted to be.

h Geoff had an uncontrollable fear of school, a fear that grew with every thought of attending it. He could only put it down to the change from primary school to secondary education. At one time he had been safe, safe inside the shell of Stanford Primary School. But now that shell had been opened, and Geoff was released from its womb and let out into the noisy, rough hell-world of Elgan Comprehensive, a world he was not ready for.

E Short story

The final extract is a complete short story. Again, the paragraphs have been jumbled up. As you read them, look for clues that tell you how to put them in the right order so that the story makes sense.

- It will help you to answer these questions *first*:

  a) What is the central character planning to do?
  b) Why has she or he been driven to this action?
  c) Who is the victim?
  d) What goes wrong?

As with many of the reading tasks in this book, this one is best tackled with a partner or in a group.

a Time was running out on him, in any case. As a lawyer who specialized in handling wills, a lot of money passed through his hands–and some of it had passed into them. A year ago he'd 'borrowed' five thousand dollars to put into something that looked a sure-fire way to double or triple the money, but he'd lost it instead. Then he'd 'borrowed' more to gamble with, in one way or another, to try to recover the first loss. Now he was behind to the tune of over thirty thousand; the shortage couldn't be hidden more than another few months and there wasn't a hope that he could replace the missing money by that time. So he had been raising all the cash he could without arousing suspicion, by carefully selling property, and by this afternoon he'd have running-away money to the tune of well over a hundred thousand dollars, enough to last him the rest of his life.

b Every little detail had been worked out, but this was the final check. Tonight at forty-six minutes past eight he'd be free, in every way. He'd picked that moment because this was his fortieth birthday and that was the exact time of day, of the evening rather, when he had been born. His mother had been an astrology fanatic, which was why the moment of his birth had been impressed on him so exactly. He wasn't superstitious himself but it had struck his sense of humour to have his new life begin at forty, to the minute.

c And they'd never catch him. He'd planned every detail of his trip, his destination, his new identity, and it was fool-proof. He'd been working on it for months. His decision to kill his wife had been a relative afterthought. The motive was simple: he hated her. But it was only after he'd come to the decision that he'd never go to jail, that he'd kill himself if he was ever picked up, that a thought struck him. Since he'd die anyway if caught he had nothing to lose in leaving a dead wife behind him instead of a living one.

d Things went smoothly at his office: by the time he went to meet his wife everything was ready. But she dawdled over drinks and dinner and he began to worry whether he could get her home by eight forty-six. It was ridiculous, he knew, but it had become important that his moment of freedom should come then and not a minute earlier or a minute later. He watched his watch.

e He'd hardly been able to keep from laughing at the appropriateness of the birthday present she'd given him (yesterday, a day ahead of time); it had been a new suitcase. She'd also talked him into celebrating his birthday by letting her meet him downtown for dinner at seven. Little did she guess how the celebration would go after that. He planned to have her home by eight forty-six and satisfy his sense of the fitness of things by making himself a widower at that exact moment. There was a practical advantage, too, in leaving her dead. If he left her alive but asleep, she'd guess what had happened and call the police when she found him gone in the morning. If he left her dead, her body would not be found that soon, possibly not for two or three days, and he'd have a much better start.

f He awoke when the alarm clock rang, but lay in bed awhile after he'd shut it off, going a final time over the plans he had made for embezzlement that day and for murder in the evening.

g Then he flicked the switch and yellow light leaped to fill the room, and, before they could see that his wife was dead and that he was holding her up, all the assembled birthday party guests shouted 'SURPRISE'!

h He would have missed it by half a minute if he'd waited till they were inside the house. But the dark of the porch of their house was perfectly safe, as safe as inside. He swung the cosh viciously once, as she stood at the front door, waiting for him to open it. He caught her before she fell and managed to hold her upright with one arm while he got the door open and then got it closed from the inside.

Answers on page 101

Now try making up some tasks of your own, similar to the ones you have just done.

- Choose a newspaper article, magazine feature or comic strip.
- Cut carefully between the paragraphs or sections, and ask a partner to try to fit them together. Mounting the pieces on some stiff card will make them easier to store and handle.

3 Reasons for reading

Information

Lots of people enjoy reading stories and magazines, but much of our reading during the day is not like story reading at all. Car maintenance, cookery, comparing the prices and quality of goods, looking up train times: all need different kinds of reading.

Sometimes you read something simply to find out one or two things. If this is the case, you don't have to read all the print word for word. You just quickly look through, or *scan* the passage until you find out what you are looking for.

These next examples will give you some practice at scanning in this way.

A The school day

- The table below gives an idea of the length of the school day in five European countries. Use it to find out as quickly as possible the answers to the questions below.

	Start of school day	Duration in hours of: morning session	midday break	afternoon session	End of school day
France					
(primary)	8.30	3	2	3	16.30
(secondary)	8.30	4	1½	3½	17.30
Italy	8.30	4	—	—	12.30
Spain					
(EGB)	9.00	3½	2½–3	2½	17.30
(instituto)	9.00	4½	2½–3	2½	18.30
Portugal	9.00	3	1½	2½	16.00
West Germany	8.00	5	—	—	13.00

a) In which country does the school day start earliest?
b) In which country does the school day end latest?
c) How long is the afternoon session in French secondary schools?
d) What time does school finish in Italy?
e) Which country's school day is most similar to our own?
f) Suggest a reason for the long lunch hour in Spanish schools.
g) What are your own thoughts on the length of the school day and school holidays? Write about this. You can use the title 'What I think of school working hours' or 'Times of the day when I work best'.

Answers on page 101

B The population explosion

From this passage, find out as quickly as you can, the following facts:
a) What was the population in 1940?
b) What factor was the more important in the rise of population in the nineteenth century
   i) the birth rate?
   ii) the death rate?
c) Who discovered vaccination?

THE POPULATION EXPLOSION

One of the most important things that happened in modern British history is that the population grew startlingly in a very short time. This began some time in the eighteenth century. Look at the graph of population from 1300 to 1900. It shows that the size of the population stayed fairly steady for several centuries. Then suddenly it began to rise dramatically. Look at the figures in the table for the population of England and Wales from 1700 onwards.

Date	Number of people
1700	about 5½ million
1800	about 9 million
1850	about 18 million
1900	about 36 million
1940	about 42 million
1970	about 48 million

You can see that the population nearly doubled in the eighteenth century, and doubled again in the next fifty years. In the fifty years after that, it doubled again!

How do we know?

Today, we know about the size of the population because of the CENSUS. This is a survey which is held every ten years to count the number of people living in the country at that time. The first proper census was held in March 1801. Before that, we are not really sure of exact figures.

In 1696, a government official named Gregory King made an estimate of the population. He based his figures on tax returns, parish registers and church records for 1695, and came up with the figure for England and Wales of 5,500,520. We still think that he was very nearly right. JOHN RICKMAN, who was in charge of the first census in 1801, worked out figures for the whole of the eighteenth century from the same kind of records. He reckoned the population of 1700 as 5,475,000.

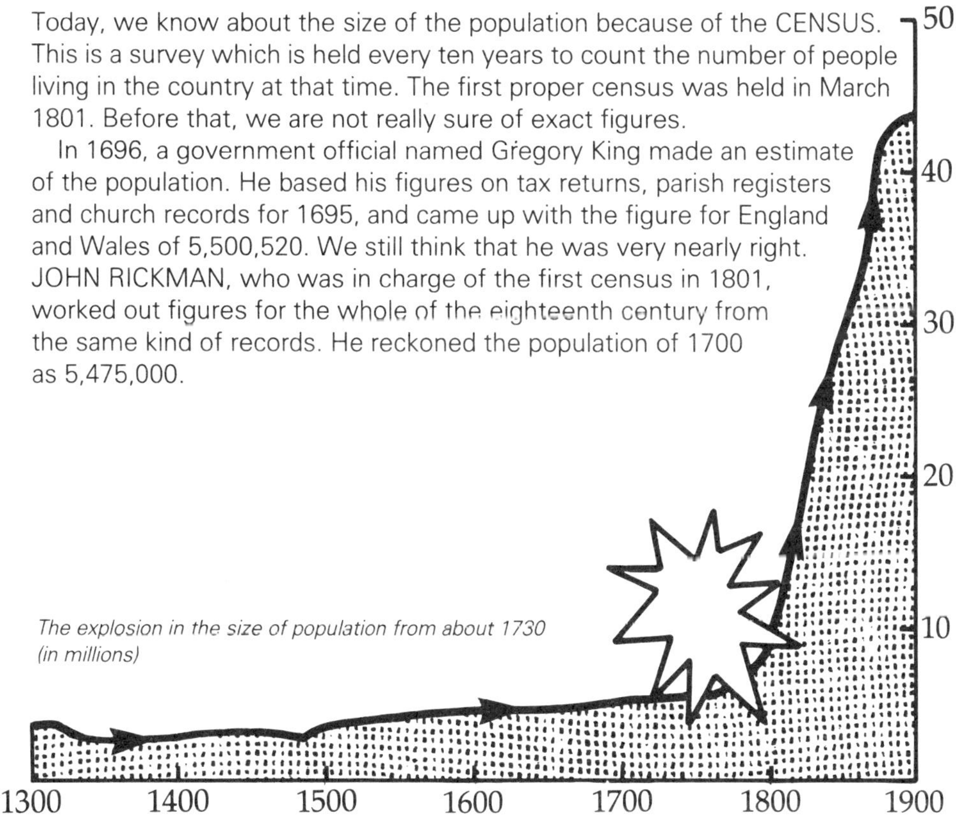

The explosion in the size of population from about 1730 (in millions)

The death rate

In order to understand the sudden rise in population, it is important to remember that the size of a population does not just depend on the number of people who are born but also the number of people who die. In the eighteenth century, the number of births (called the BIRTH RATE) did begin to rise slightly, but that was not the most important reason for this particular growth in population. The real change came in the number of people who died, or the DEATH RATE. The death rate began to fall continuously from 1700 onwards, except for one short time at the start of the nineteenth century. Far fewer young children were dying, and far more people were living longer, this was what made the population grow so much.

Why did the death rate decline in the eighteenth century?

There is no easy answer to this question. We do know that people's health was very bad up to this time, and about half of all children died before the age of five. Most people were very lucky to live into what we would call middle age. Dirt, disease, lack of medical knowledge, poor food, bad living conditions–all these were the enemies of long life.

Then people's health slowly began to improve in the eighteenth century, because of other changes that were happening in Britain. Here is a list of the main changes which made the death rate fall.

1 Improvements in FARMING were beginning to produce bigger crops of a better quality.
2 As TRANSPORT improved within Britain, fresh food became more easily available in every part of the country, and often it became cheaper. This certainly improved people's health.
3 TRADE with countries overseas was increasing, and this also brought better food to people in this country. Trade brought in goods like COTTON as well, and this was healthier to wear than the old, thick woollen materials that had nearly always been worn before.
4 As INDUSTRY grew, people often began to earn higher wages to spend on their food, clothing and housing, and these things often became cheaper. But at the same time the conditions in towns were so dirty that the Industrial Revolution did not really have a good effect on people's health. Only from the middle of the nineteenth century did Government action help to improve PUBLIC HEALTH.

5 Improvements in MEDICINE may have helped people to live longer, but not really as early as the eighteenth century. It was to be some time before doctors were sure of the cures for diseases, and although several more hospitals were being built in the eighteenth century, they were still dirty and overcrowded. Edward Jenner's discovery of VACCINATION did not happen until 1796.

Now that you have got a rough idea about the content of the passage, answer these more detailed questions. This will require slower and more thoughtful reading.

d) What is a census?
e) What were some of the reasons for people's poor health prior to the eighteenth century?
f) How did trade help to improve people's health?
g) Did any medical improvements occur in the early eighteenth century to slow down the death rate?
h) The graph showing the population explosion is not very good. It is not clearly labelled, and its information contradicts facts mentioned elsewhere in the passage. See if you can track down these faults. Then draw up a better graph of your own.

Answers on page 101

C Airline

The chart below shows you the distances between the seven major airports in Canada and a range of other airports throughout the world.

- Have a look at it to make sure you understand it. Then answer the questions on page 33.

AIRLINE DISTANCES IN STATUTE MILES/KILOMETRES

SM / KMS	ACAPULCO	AMSTERDAM	ARUBA	ATHENS	BARBADOS	CARTAGENA	COPENHAGEN	DUBLIN	DUBROVNIK	FRANKFURT	HONOLULU	LONDON	LOS ANGELES	MALAGA	MANCHESTER	MEXICO CITY	MIAMI	NASSAU	PARIS	PRESTWICK
CALGARY	2690	4452	3622	5775	4096	3547	4454	4094	5357	4676	3121	4381	1205	3024	4208	2333	2482	2805	4583	4037
	4329	7165	5829	9293	6592	5709	7163	6589	8621	7526	5023	7050	1939	8085	6774	3755	3994	4514	7376	6497
EDMONTON	2845	4318	3689	5635	4260	3630	4313	3967	5220	4541	3191	4252	1367	4917	4079	2600	2551	2861	4454	3906
	4579	6949	5937	9069	6856	5842	6941	6385	8400	7308	5135	5843	2201	7913	6566	4184	4105	4604	7169	6286
MONTREAL	2485	3419	2303	4733	2387	2434	3604	2963	4309	3636	4902	3258	2469	3543	3119	2307	1406	1425	2983	3102
	3999	5502	3707	7617	3841	3918	5800	4768	6935	5852	7889	5243	3973	5701	5020	3713	2263	2293	3432	4992
OTTAWA	2413	3498	2290	4817	2421	2408	3677	3044	4388	3716	4815	3340	2373	3536	3200	2233	1428	1403	3612	3063
	3883	5629	3686	7752	3895	3875	5918	4899	7061	5981	7748	5375	3820	5852	5150	3594	2298	2258	5652	4929
TORONTO	2200	3721	2260	5041	2438	2309	3892	3267	4614	3939	4638	3564	2170	3857	3422	2018	1235	1292	3742	3284
	3541	5988	3638	8113	3923	3716	6264	5258	7426	6340	7464	5735	3492	6207	5507	3248	1988	2079	6022	5285
VANCOUVER	2595	4787	3927	6085	3982	3814	4758	4449	5678	5006	2703	4731	1080	5418	4556	2448	2791	3321	4923	4382
	4176	7704	6320	9793	6480	6139	7667	7160	9138	8057	4350	7614	1738	8719	7332	3940	4492	5345	7923	7052
WINNIPEG	2344	4035	3010	5384	3010	2995	4108	3630	4955	4262	3806	3928	1537	4446	3764	2146	1889	2160	4116	3601
	3772	6494	4844	8665	4844	4820	6611	5842	7974	6861	6125	6321	2474	7156	6058	3454	3040	3476	6624	5795

a) Why are the airports listed in this particular order?
b) How many miles is it from Ottawa to:
   i) Athens
   ii) Dublin
   iii) Paris?
c) How many kilometres is it from Dublin to:
   i) Winnipeg
   ii) Ottawa?
d) Which is furthest from Vancouver?
   i) Amsterdam
   ii) Copenhagen
   iii) Manchester
e) Which British airport is nearest to Edmonton?
f) Use an atlas to find out which of the Canadian airports is:
   i) furthest north
   ii) nearest the Pacific Ocean

Answers on page 102

D School textbook

When we look through a book in a library or bookshop, or pick up an information leaflet which has been poked through our door, we don't read it all. We get enough information from a few important words, headings or pictures to decide whether it is worth a closer reading.

This is sometimes called *skimming*.

- The next extract is from a school textbook. Find out what it is about by skimming through it quickly to decide the answer to question (a).

a) Is this passage taken from
   i) an English textbook?
   ii) a French textbook?
   iii) a History textbook?
   iv) an RE textbook?
   v) a Physics textbook?

Workmen were used to toiling long hours for low wages before the Industrial Revolution. Most of them accepted their fate as part of the natural order of things. But the beginnings of factory industry brought numbers of them together in one place. They now began to develop a sense of unity and common purpose, for they were more aware of the weakness and inferiority of their position than their fathers and grandfathers had been. As the new 'working class' became established in the industrial towns, its members began to realize the power they could possess if they acted *together* instead of separately. Thus they organized themselves in various ways to bring about improvements in their standard of living.

Before the Industrial Revolution there were no trade unions in the modern sense. However, during the eighteenth century, trade clubs had become established in many towns. These contained workmen in a particular trade or occupation and usually met regularly at a local public house, many of which still bear their names today, like 'The Bricklayers' Arms'. Good company and strong ale were the first priority, but they also attended to more serious matters–such as accepting new apprentices, and putting aside a penny or twopence a week to help those out of work. These taverns also became 'places of call', where employers could recruit extra workmen. Occasionally, when their employers threatened to reduce rates of pay or refused them increases when the cost of living rose, members banded together to defend their interests. As early as 1720, thousands of London tailors joined together in this way against their masters.

It was a short step from the activities of trade clubs to full-scale trade unions. These began when a number of clubs 'combined to fight for a common aim'. In the eighteenth century, trade unions usually arose to deal with a particular problem and then broke up when it was settled. Their most powerful weapon was a threatened stoppage of work, or strike. Workmen realized that if they all asked for the same thing, and refused to go on with their jobs unless they got it, they would be in a good bargaining position with their employers. Faced with loss of business and possible ruin, employers were usually forced to reach some sort of agreement with the union. Strikes were quite common in the late eighteenth century. Among the most successful were those of the London tailors, who managed to raise their wages by a quarter (from 18*s* 9*d* to 25*s*) as a result of strike action between 1775 and 1800. The naval mutinies of 1797 were really strikes against low pay and unsatisfactory working conditions.

b) Which of these statements is the best description of what the passage is about?
   i) It is an attack on employers.
   ii) It is a description of poor working conditions.
   iii) It is about the influence of public houses on trade unions.
   iv) It is an account of the development of trade unions.
   v) It is about strikes between 1775 and 1800.

   You may need to read the passage quickly again to check that you are right.

Now that you have got an idea of what the passage is about, answer these more detailed questions.

c) How easy was it to make up your mind about questions (a) and (b)? Write down three things that helped you to decide what kind of a textbook the passage came from.
d) If you saw a pub called *The Clothworkers' Arms*, what would it tell you about its history?
e) Say what the author meant by the phrases in italic as they are used in the passage:
   i) Most of them accepted their fate *as part of the natural order of things* (lines 2–3)
   ii) members banded together *to defend their interests* (lines 23–4)
   iii) they would be *in a good bargaining position* with their employers (lines 32–3)

Answers on page 102

E Origami

Following instructions is another practical kind of reading which most of us have to do. The real test of whether you have read a set of instructions properly is how far you succeed in doing what they tell you to do.

- Here is a set of instructions showing you how to make a dog, using a piece of paper. (Making paper models is called *origami*.) Follow the instructions and see if you get it right.

1 Use a square of paper. Fold two corners together to mark the centre line; then open.

2 Fold the two upper sides to the centre line.

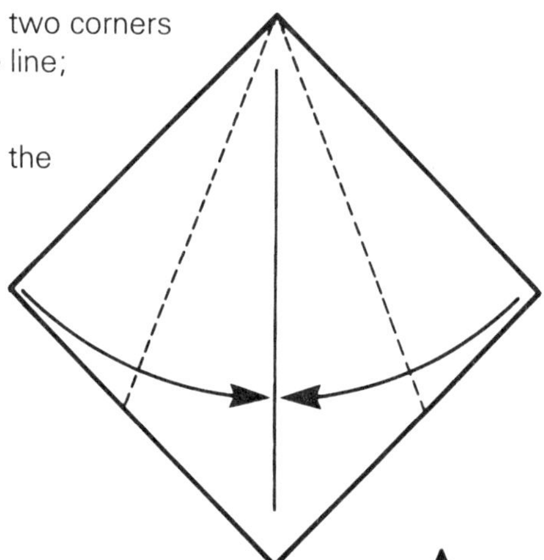

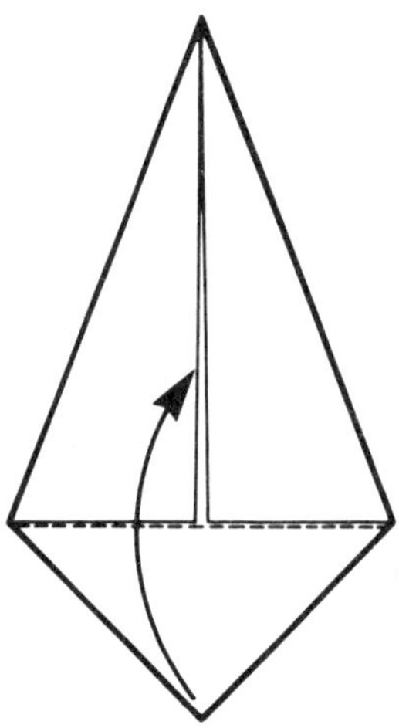

3 Fold up the triangular flap.

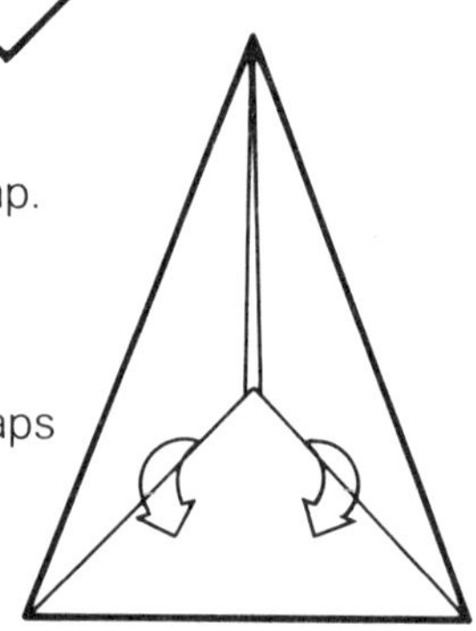

4 Bring the concealed flaps to the front.

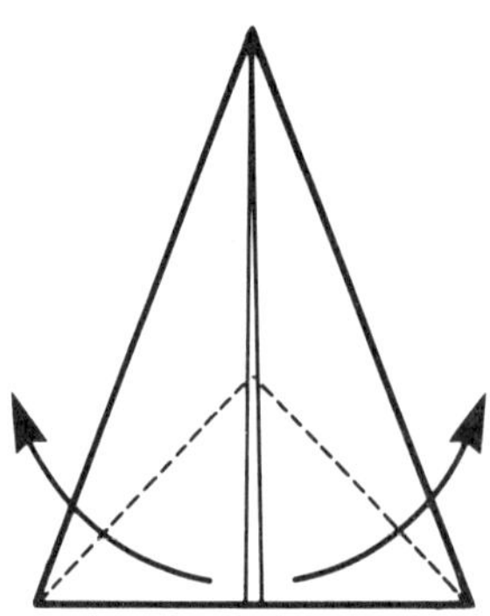

5 Fold up these two flaps (fold lines run along the sides of the concealed triangular flap). Then turn the paper over.

6 Fold the bottom corners to the centre line.

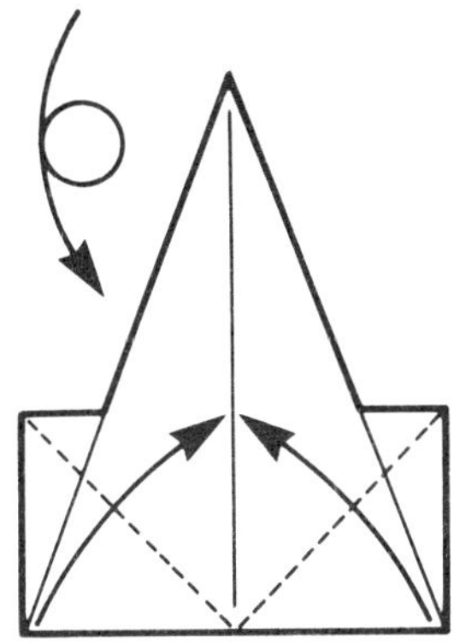

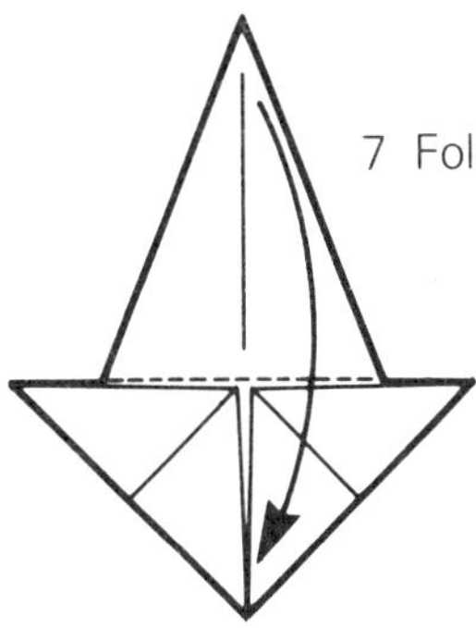

7 Fold the top flap down.

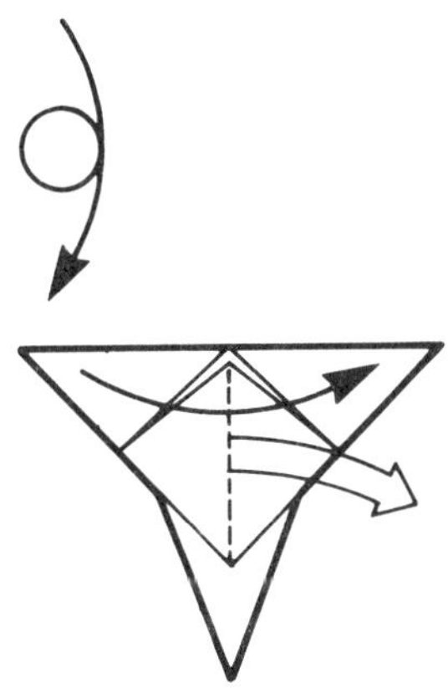

8 Turn the paper over. Fold the model in half; at the same time pull forward and collapse the middle flap.

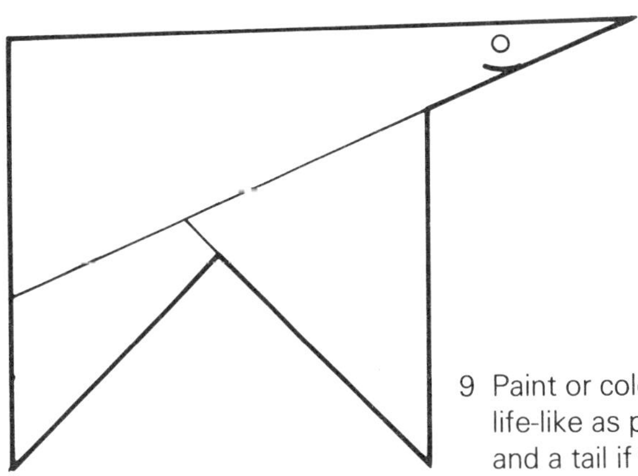

9 Paint or colour the model to make it as life-like as possible. You can add ears and a tail if you like.

4 What's next?

Information

All of us tell stories in everyday life; sometimes they are true, sometimes not. Mostly though, they are a kind of mixture of the two. For instance, we may be telling someone about the dreadful day we've had or about some terrifically funny thing that happened at school. In each case we'll select, exaggerate and organize the events to make them interesting to our listeners.

We also like listening to people telling stories and part of the pleasure is that we can use our imagination and experience of life to enter into what they are talking about. that's why serials on TV or in magazines are so popular. We get to know the characters involved and we can think about what they are going to say and do. We may even be able to predict what is going to happen next.

The extracts in the next section are parts of stories. Your task is to read each one carefully, use your imagination to see the situation and people involved and then use your reading skill to answer the questions. (In most cases there are no 'right' answers because each of us will read the story in a slightly different way.)

A The shark

➔

- Read the following story one section at a time. Stop when you have finished each section and guess what the answer is to the question printed below it. You will probably notice that you already thought of the question yourself and maybe you've got a fair idea of the answer. In fact, it is difficult to read a good story without questioning the writer in this way.

THE SHARK

The shark was hungry again. It was always hungry and spent its life continually searching for food. It scavenged remorselessly and ate anything that came its way. Best of all, it liked meat: good, red meat. Living meat where the blood still pulsated.

Like most of its species it was aggressive without reason. All of its Australian breed were ferocious to the extreme, quite without fear and a terror to all in the sea except the killer whale.

The shark wanted meat–now. It swam around in agitation, its progress a small circle, its senses tantalized by the scent. Somewhere, not far away, was meat, living meat, too!

The current wafted the blood scent nearer and the shark pinpointed the meat's direction. With a powerful thrust of its tail, it reversed its circling and shot away to one side. Small, piggy eyes searched. Keen nostrils dissected the sea and homed the shark on a correct course.

With unerring precision, the shark increased speed, its progress effortless. It cut through the water with dorsal and tail fins beautifully balanced, giving a rapid, streamlined progression.

What prey do you think the shark is after?

The swimmer was preoccupied with the matter at hand. He had one spear left for his gun and no fish yet to show for his sport. He was so totally occupied with hunting that he had not felt the tear in his skin where the coral had snagged his leg. The pain was non-existent, the skin cut small. The blood loss minute–but enough to reach the shark's uncanny nostrils and trigger off a hunt.

The hunter was about to turn into the hunted. The vicious shark with its puny brain against the intelligent man with his weak body.

The shark decreased speed and slowed into a cruising circle while it considered the situation. The blood scent tantalized its ravenous appetite but, as yet, the shark was not angry enough to attack without surveying the scene. It wanted to weigh up the opposition. Its temper was not quite demoniacal. Once that stage had been reached the opposition's strength was of no consequence. Only the attack and feast would matter.

The swimmer saw a fat fish move nearby and carefully lined up his gun. One finger took up the trigger's slack. He sighted carefully, making allowance for the water's deflection.

What will the swimmer do with the one spear he has left?

He was on the verge of firing when death rippled cold fingers along the length of his spine. In the warm, tropical sea his body shivered with a chill deep enough to penetrate his guts. His finger came off the trigger. The fish swam lazily away. The shark appeared in view on its narrowing circle.

The swimmer felt gall rise up in his throat. He almost gagged on his mouthpiece as his grey eyes stared mesmerized at the sheer size of the whaler shark. The most wicked of all the sharks in the Australian coastal waters and this was the grand daddy of them all!

What should he do? He had his one spear left and a mere fifteen minutes' oxygen in his cylinders. This gave him precious little margin for safety.

He was only at a depth of twenty feet and the shoreline was not much farther away than that, but the greatest danger would be in the ascent. Two retreating human feet would goad any shark into a frenzied attack let alone a whaler, which usually required little excuse to kill a man.

The shark's circle decreased as the thin vapour trail of blood tickled the beast's ever-shrunken stomach. The beady eyes decided this meat would be good and easy to take. The sweet allure of the blood was triggering the temper fuse in the shark's small brain into a state of explosive ferocity. Here was the wanted meat! Good living meat! Now to take it!

What would you not do if you were the swimmer?

The dorsal fin altered its angle a fraction. The shark's body changed course. The great rudder of a tail thrashed left and then right sending the huge torpedo shaped body forward in the first probing attack.

The swimmer circled on the axis. Spear gun at the ready. His heart beats drummed in his ears. They reached such a pitch that it required rigid self-discipline to concentrate and to breath in the steady rhythm necessary to gain the best from his oxygen cylinders. He must not panic! It would be fatal to swim wildly or breathe too quickly–but the time! Those precious minutes ticking away. The shore was so near–and yet so far!

The shark churned straight at the swimmer. Three feet away it rolled on its back. Exposing a pale-coloured belly. Gills and slit, open jaws and rows of razor-sharp retracting teeth. Terrible teeth which, once they had gripped anything, could not let go without taking flesh with them.

The swimmer had anticipated the shark's classical attack. At the last second he thrust back with his flippered feet and moved out of range. He took care to keep the spear gun before his body. His fingers itched to fire. His mind ordered restraint. This one shot must be perfect. The shark had a tough skin. There would be no second chance.

Does the swimmer kill the shark with his last shot?

Baulked by the swimmer's action the shark churned past, turned, and charged again. The great jaws opened, slashing at an arm. The spear gun jabbed hard in the shark's eye. The sudden pain blunted the whaler's venom temporarily.

The swimmer anxiously looked at his watch. Seven minutes left! He must surface soon! He scanned the sea, peering intently through his goggles and thought he saw other shapes appearing in the distance.

What are these 'other shapes'?

He made up his mind. It was now or never! He lined up his spear gun, finger again on the trigger. The next charge would be the last–for himself or the shark.

The shark broke from its circle and headed into the attack again, equally determined to end this before other predators appeared and expected a part of the meal.

The swimmer kept himself as still as possible, flippered feet moved gently, maintaining an upright stance in the water. The shark was a terrifying sight as it headed as straight as an arrow but the swimmer was suddenly unafraid now. The time for that was past.

The spear gun was lifted an inch. A sight was taken on the head. As seconds ticked by the swimmer felt cool anger sweep through him. The shark bellied over again for its usual attack. This was it!

With steady hands the swimmer pressed the trigger. The spear shot free and plunged in the shark's exposed under-belly. It disappeared half-way up its length.

The shark jerked sideways, rolling over wildly, trying to snap at the thing lodged in its vitals. The water heaved and boiled as the huge tail thrashed in wild contortions.

The swimmer fled. He thrust upwards. A snap glance at his watch had shown just two minutes' air left. He discarded his gun. Peered around as arms and legs pushed him to the surface. There were other forms appearing. Ugly, dark torpedoes who were moving in. Converging on a point where the water was stained and boiled in a cauldron.

His head broke surface and the swimmer flung himself into the fast and powerful Australian trudgeon crawl. The shore! Those rocks. Ten feet to go! Was anything coming after his feet? He spat out his useless mouthpiece and gasped wildly. His lungs straining under the cruel effort required for such a pace.

Does he make it to the shore?

One sun-tanned hand grasped a rock. The other pulled. Within four seconds he was out of the water and safe on the rock of the shoreline. He collapsed. His body shuddered from goggled eyes to rubber-shod feet.

Slowly he sat up and slipped the useless oxygen cylinders from his brown back. He rubbed his neck and only then noticed the cut on his leg. A wry grimace crossed his face as understanding dawned. It had been such a near thing.

Twenty feet away and ten feet below the surface the water spewed in a mixture of white, blue and red. Objects churned frantically until the sea appeared to be having a paroxysm.

The swimmer stood and watched. The pack of tiger sharks were as relentless as the whaler had been. Blood flowed! Meat was for the taking! They converged upon the dying whaler and tore him to shreds.

Once again the hunter had become the hunted.

How many times were you right in guessing what would happen?

B Answer

This is a complete short story with only the last paragraph missing. It is set in the far future when man has developed a powerful computer. As the story opens, the final connections are being made. . . .

Dwar Ev ceremoniously soldered the final connection with gold. The eyes of a dozen television cameras watched him and the subether bore throughout the universe a dozen pictures of what he was doing.

He straightened and nodded to Dwar Reyn, then moved to a position beside the switch that would complete the contact when he threw it. The switch that would connect, all at once, all of the monster computing machines of all the populated planets in the universe–ninety-six billion planets–into the super-circuit that would connect them all into one supercalculator, one cybernetics machine that would combine all the knowledge of all the galaxies. Dwar Reyn spoke briefly to the watching and listening trillions. Then after a moment's silence he said, 'Now, Dwar Ev.'

Dwar Ev threw the switch.There was a mighty hum, the surge of power from ninety-six billion planets. Lights flashed and quieted along the miles-long panel.

Dwar Ev stepped back and drew a deep breath. 'The honour of asking the first questions is yours, Dwar Reyn.' 'Thank you,' said Dwar Reyn. 'It shall be a question which no single cybernetics machine has been able to answer.' He turned to face the machine.

a) What are the meanings of the following words as used in the passage?
   i) ceremoniously
   ii) cybernetics
   iii) galaxies
b) In your opinion, what was the question 'which no single cybernetics machine has been able to answer'? Make up your own suitable question.
c) What do you imagine was the computer's answer to that question? Write down a suitable answer.
d) How do you think the story ends?
e) Read the last part of the story on page 103. Do you think the original version is a good one or do you prefer your own? Give reasons for your answer.

Answers on page 102

C Do you read me?

Read the following passage which is also the first part of a story. Even though it is fairly short we have quite a good idea of the characters involved and what sort of story it is.

It was the custom to bring back yearly reports, signed, at the beginning of the autumn term, to prove that they had been shown to parents, or at least to a competent forger. Fenton, the Fifth Year tutor, was At Home in his office on Friday morning to receive them. When Rodney King clinked in with his report and laid it on the desk under Fenton's nose, Fenton looked at it, looked at Rodney, crossed his knees, folded his hands, and sat back with the air of a man who has prepared a little speech.

'It's a good one, in most respects, especially for Art and Design, I see. A+, eh? Parents pleased?'

Rodney nodded.

'Only there's this nasty little rider here, to the effect that you have difficulty in communicating. What does that mean, do you think?'

Rodney shrugged.

'It could mean that you don't say much for yourself. Might that be the trouble? A bit of a loner, are you? No close friends?'

Rodney made a non-committal noise through the slit between his front teeth.

'Your written work's excellent – no complaints from anyone about that – but you've got to learn to verbalize. You'll be doing English, this year. What's going to happen when you come to the oral?'

Rodney's hand described a gesture that dealt dismissively with the English oral. He took a step backward to indicate that he thought the interview might usefully be concluded.

'It's no good relying on badges to do your communicating for you,' Fenton said. 'I mean, it's very reassuring to see you covered in slogans for Nuclear Disarmament and Rock against Racism, but any idiot can pin on a badge. How many have you got?'

Rodney was moved to verbalize. 'Seventy-three.'

'And are you wearing them all?'

'Yes, Sir.'

'Look, King, don't feel that I'm criticizing gratuitously, but when the Headmaster abolished school uniform for the Fifth and Sixth Forms, I doubt if he intended you to come to school in armour plate. You look like a pearly king under a microscope. The people who sit behind you don't do any work; they spend all their time reading your badges.'

'I could move to the back,' Rodney offered, helpfully.

'Don't think of it,' Fenton said. 'We might lose touch with you altogether. Just move the badges from the rear of that cut-price Biggles outfit – and the sleeves. Be selective, King. Use your designer's eye. Just a few, here and there, tastefully arranged, should be quite aesthetically pleasing. We'll get the message – one message at a time. OK?'

Rodney returned to school on Monday with his bomber jacket feeling several pounds lighter, and ran into Fenton in the corridor where he was pinning a sheet of foolscap to the Fifth Year notice board.

'Book Fair,' said Fenton. 'October 8th, St Stephen's Hall. Want to come? Sign here.'

Rodney wove a deprecating pattern with his toes on the vinyl tiles, and the collar of his jacket rose about his ears.

'Oh, King, what eloquent shoulders you do have,' Fenton said. 'I'll take silence for consent. There, you can put your name down right at the top of the list. I suppose that elaborate routine is meant to suggest that you have nothing to write with? Tough titty,' said Fenton, whipping out his biro, and writing Rodney's name in cock-eyed capitals at the head of the paper. 'No one,' Fenton observed, 'would know that you hadn't written it yourself. And now I'll tell you something you'll really like. At this book fair they will have real live authors – and a badge-making machine.'

The lower forms went down to the Book Fair in supervised groups. The Fifth Year, as befitted the enormous strides that they had made in self-discipline during the summer holidays, were left to find their own way. Rodney attached himself wordlessly to a sauntering cluster comprising the visual cream of his class: Eddie Hobson known as Hobbers, and his three young ladies: Anna Miles, Katy Matthews, and Liz Salkey, the one with the eyes, the one with the ankles, the one with absolutely everything in between and all of it, by popular repute, promised to horrible Hobbers. Rodney suspected that they considered themselves too pretty to be seen associating with his own plain person, but knowing that if they told him to go away he would neither answer nor go away, they allowed him to slouch behind them to the hall.

Inside, they looked round in disdain.

'It's all kids' stuff,' Katy said. 'Little baby books and posters. Fenton's pulled a fast one on us.'

'All this way and nothing to read,' mourned Hobbers, who had never yet been caught in possession of a book. 'Can't even read old King these days, since Fenton debadged him. I bet you took the filthy ones off, King.'

'He never had any filthy ones,' Anna said.

'He did,' said Hobbers, quietly, 'only he's so thick he doesn't know they were filthy.' Liz, lovely Liz, said nothing at all.

Rodney set off round the hall. There were five live authors, all looking repellently like teachers, several thousand books, a man flogging literary T-shirts, and the badge-making machine. The queue for badges stretched down one side of the hall, and Rodney attached himself to the tail of it, feeling like Gulliver in Lilliput among so many first school children, all squeaking like unoiled roller skates. Fenton had reminded everyone to bring money with which to buy books, to be signed by the live authors. Rodney had brought two pounds with which he bought ten badge blanks. The little kids all round him were scrawling their names in orange or turquoise, and drawing Dracula, with bats. Rodney brought his A+ for Art and Design into play. He heard Liz addressing Hobbers.

'Let's both get a badge made. I'll have your name and you have mine.'

'Get out of it,' said the gallant Hobbers. 'I might get taken for King in a bad light.'

'I'll make you a badge, Liz,' Rodney said, suddenly, before he had time to lose courage. 'What would you like?'

'You stick to scribbling on your own walls, beautiful,' Hobbers said obscurely, with throaty threatening noises, and Liz was hauled away, badgeless.

a) What do we learn about the personality of Fenton? Make a list of different aspects of his character and how the reader gets to know each one. Set it out like this:
   i) Mr. Fenton likes using long words.
   Evidence: he says 'don't feel I'm criticising gratuitously'.
b) Do you think Fenton is a good teacher? Give reasons for your opinion.
c) What do you notice about Rodney and the way he acts? Why do you think he wears so many badges?
d) Is there anything to laugh at in the way the story is told?
e) In the last part of the extract what do you notice about the way Hobbers and Rodney act towards Liz?
f) When you've read the passage carefully, make up your own version of the rest of the story, making it fit the start you have been given. (The original story goes on for about another 810 words. You can find it on page 104. How does it compare with yours?')

Answers on page 103

D Examination day

Read the following passage. It is the beginning of a short story. When you have read it you will notice it raises a lot of questions.

EXAMINATION DAY

The Jordans never spoke of the exam, not until their son, Dickie, was twelve years old. It was on his birthday that Mrs Jordan first mentioned the subject in his presence, and the anxious manner of her speech caused her husband to answer sharply.

'Forget about it,' he said. 'He'll do all right.'

They were at the breakfast table, and the boy looked up from his plate curiously. He was an alert-eyed youngster, with flat blond hair and a quick, nervous manner. He didn't understand what the sudden tension was about, but he did know that today was his birthday, and he wanted harmony above all. Somewhere in the little apartment there were wrapped, beribboned packages waiting to be opened, and in the tiny wall-kitchen, something warm and sweet was being prepared in the automatic stove. He wanted the day to be happy, and the moistness of his mother's eyes, the scowl on his father's face, spoiled the mood of fluttering expectation with which he had greeted the morning.

'What exam?' he asked.

His mother looked at the tablecloth. 'It's just a sort of Government intelligence test they give children at the age of twelve. You'll be taking it next week. It's nothing to worry about.'

'You mean a test like in school?'

'Something like that, 'his father said, getting up from the table. 'Go and read your comics, Dickie.' The boy rose and wandered towards that part of the living room which had been 'his' corner since infancy. He fingered the topmost comic of the stack, but seemed uninterested in the colourful squares of fast-paced action. He wandered towards the window, and peered gloomily at the veil of mist that shrouded the glass.

'Why did it have to rain today?' he said. 'Why couldn't it rain tomorrow?'

His father, now slumped into an armchair with the Government newspaper, rattled the sheets in vexation. 'Because it just did, that's all. Rain makes the grass grow.'

'Why, Dad?'

'Because it does, that's all.'

Dickie puckered his brow. 'What makes it green, though? The grass?'

'Nobody knows, 'his father snapped, then immediately regretted his abruptness.

Later in the day, it was birthday time again. His mother beamed as she handed over the gaily-coloured packages, and even his father managed a grin and a rumple-of-the-hair. He kissed his mother and shook hands gravely with his father. Then the birthday cake was brought forth, and the ceremonies concluded.

An hour later, seated by the window, he watched the sun force its way between the clouds.

'Dad,' he said, 'how far away is the sun?'

'Five thousand miles,' his father said.

a) Why do you think the Government has set an 'exam' for twelve-year olds? What might happen to Dickie when the result is known? Why are his parents so worried about it?
b) What sort of a boy is Dickie?
c) Why is the Government (with a capital 'G') mentioned twice? Do you find anything strange in this?
d) The sun is about ninety million miles from the earth. Why do you think Dickie's father says it is five thousand miles away?
e) Now make up a version of the story's ending which fits in with your answers to these kinds of questions.
f) Read the original ending to the story on page 106 and compare it with your own. Which one did you prefer and why?

Answers on page 106

E A lot to learn

- The last extract in this section is a very short one. Read the passage which is taken from the very beginning of the story. (The whole story only takes up less than a whole printed page.)

A LOT TO LEARN

The Materializer was completed.

Ned Quinn stood back, wiped his hands, and admired the huge bank of dials, lights and switches. Several years and many fortunes had gone into his project. Finally it was ready.

Ned placed the metal skullcap on his head and plugged the wires into the control panel. He turned the switch to ON and spoke: 'Pound coin.'

There was a whirring sound. In the Receiver a piece of metal appeared. Ned inspected it. Real.

'Martini,' he said.

A whirring sound. A puddle formed in the Receiver. Ned cursed silently. He had a lot to learn.

'A bottle of beer,' he said.

The whirring sound was followed by the appearance of the familiar brown bottle. Ned tasted the contents and grinned.

Chuckling, he experimented further.

a) What does the 'materializer' actually do?
b) What mistake does Ned Quinn make about the Martini?
c) Why do you think the story is called *A Lot To Learn*?
d) Write your own ending to the story and compare it with the original printed on page 108. It should be about 70 words.

Answers on page 108

5 Keeping alert

Information

Often, writers are trying to give us advice, to alert us to things we should know about, or even to change our opinions and beliefs.

This kind of writing deserves careful reading since we may need to follow a line of argument, pick out the main ideas, weigh up any evidence, and, sometimes, draw together or compare information from different pages or books.

These activities will help you to keep alert in some of these ways and to work out, through close reading, what a writer is really saying.

A Lightning

What would you do if you were caught in a violent electrical storm?

Some of the **advice** below is true, some of it is partly true, and some is dangerously false.

➔

- To find out which is which, read the passage carefully. When you have done this go through each statement and write down TRUE, FALSE or PARTLY TRUE. If it is only partly true, explain why.
- You may already know some of the answers. In that case check that the writer of the passage agrees with you.
- When you have finished, discuss your answers with a partner. If you have any disagreements, look back at the passage and discuss them.

Advice

a) If your hair stands on end and your eyebrows are tingling, you are in immediate danger.

b) Cave entrances and steep hillsides are comparatively safe places to be in an electrical storm.
c) Crouching beneath a ledge of jutting granite is very dangerous because lightning can strike the overhang and send the rock crashing on your head.
d) It is perfectly safe to be in the middle of a field as long as you lie down.
e) Rubber boots provide added safety in a storm.
f) Never shelter under a tree. This is very dangerous.
g) If your car is struck by lightning you could be frizzled alive like meat in an oven.
h) You can calculate how far away lightning is, because each second between the lightning and the thunder represents about a mile in distance.
i) It is quite safe to carry metal equipment like ice axes in a violent storm.
j) If you have to shelter under a tree then choose a poplar or elm.

LIGHTNING

It is not necessary to jettison metal pieces of equipment like ice axes, karabiners, rucksacks and crampons. They do not attract lightning any more than you do, and you could meet serious trouble through throwing away vital gear.

However, you should know the places to stay away from when lightning rends the sky . . . and the spots to head for where safety is virtually assured.

Worst places

Beneath oak, poplar or elm trees, whose sap blows up if struck by a lightning flash.

Anywhere where you are the tallest and most obvious silhouette against open country . . . and the lightning flash is only five seconds before the crash of thunder (divide the number of seconds by five to find how many miles away the lightning is striking): in this case it is only one mile away and therefore far too near for comfort.

Beneath an isolated tree, no matter how tall. Or below any other high-standing targets which, by their lonesome height, attract lightning flashes (the Empire State Building in New York City has been struck many times a year because it stands so much higher than the other tall buildings around).

Cave entrances: they pull lightning because of the ionization of the air at the cave mouth.

Mountain skylines–especially in overcast, rainy weather.

Steep hillsides, rock face cracks and rock overhangs . . . steer well clear of these spots even though they would appear to give welcome shelter. For example, if you crouch beneath a roof formed by a ledge of jutting granite, then you are in a very dangerous position. A flash of lightning could strike the projecting lip of the overhang and then, at once, begin arcing to the ground beneath. You, trapped in the middle, will be in the position of being electrocuted in a giant sparking plug. Yet, it was the projection of the overhang which attracted the lightning in the first place.

Best places

In the midst of dense woods where all the trees are more or less the same height–you would have to be very unlucky for it to strike the tree under which you are immediately sheltering.

Inside a car whose surface distributes the lightning through its metal and then guides it back to earth.

Inside any building which has a 'low profile' because it is among other buildings in the immediate neighbourhood. And is of much the same height.

Lying on your stomach in the middle of a field, and thereby presenting a low profile of yourself. If you were standing up, you would then be in one of the worst places.

Sitting on an open scree slope well below mountain crests and well away from any rock faces–knees up with your hands in your lap. Crouch, squatting on the balls of your feet, if you have rubber-soled boots.

Anywhere flat where you can lie, crouch or sit. Do not worry if your ice axe is making a buzzing sound, your hair is standing on end, your eyebrows are tingling and there are blue flashes all over the ground in front of your eyes. So long as you keep low and on the level, the big forks of lightning will most likely give you the miss even though the immediate atmosphere is highly charged with electricity.

- Now answer these questions:

a) What are the meanings of these words and phrases as used in the passage?
   i) jettison
   ii) virtually assured
   iii) low profile
   iv) scree slope

b) Write your own advice for Worst places and Best places, choosing one of these topics:

i) hang-gliding
iii) camping
iii) swimming in the sea, rivers or lakes

Draw the advice together in two lists. Again, you will probably get a lot more ideas if you work with a partner.

Answers on page 108

B The blitz

The following extract is taken from an account of life in London during the bombing of the Second World War–the 'blitz', as it was called.

- Read it carefully.

STORIES OF THE BLITZ

LONDON, *July 10, 1943*–People who try to tell you what the blitz was like in London start with fire and explosion and then almost *invariably* end up with some very tiny detail which crept in and set and became the symbol of the whole thing for them. Again and again this happens in conversations. It is as though the mind could not take in the terror and the noise of the bombs and the general horror and so fastened on something small and *comprehensible* and ordinary. Everyone who was in London during the blitz wants to describe it, wants to solidify, if only for himself, something of that terrible time.

'It's the glass,' says one man, 'the sound in the morning of the broken glass being swept up, the vicious, flat tinkle. That is the thing I remember more than anything else, that constant sound of broken glass being swept up on the pavements. My dog broke a window the other day and my wife swept up the glass and a cold shiver went over me. It was a moment before I could trace the reason for it.'

You are going to dine at a small restaurant. There is a ruin across the street from the place, a jagged, destroyed stone house. Your companion says, 'On one of the nights I had an engagement to have dinner with a lady at this very place. She was to meet me here. I got here early and then a bomb hit that one.' He points to the ruin. 'I went out in the street. You could see plainly, the fires lighted the whole city. That front wall was spilled into the street. You could see the front of a cab sticking out from the pile of fallen stone. Thrown clear, right at my feet as I came out of the door, was one pale blue evening slipper. The toe of it was pointing right at me.'

Another points up at a wall; the building is gone, but there are five fireplaces, one above another, straight up the wall. He points to the topmost fireplace. 'This was a high-explosive bomb,' he says. 'This is on my way to work. You know, for six months there was a pair of long stockings hanging in front of that fireplace. They must have been pinned up. They hung there for months, just as they had been put up to dry.'

'I was passing Hyde Park,' says a man, 'when a big raid came over. I went down into the gutter. Always did that when you couldn't get a shelter. I saw a great tree, one like those, jump into the air and fall on its side not so far from me–right there where that scoop is in the ground. And then a sparrow fell in the gutter right beside me. It was dead all right. Concussion kills birds easily. For some reason I picked it up and held it for a long time. There was no blood on it or anything like that. I took it home with me. Funny thing, I had to throw it right away.'

One night, when the bombs screamed and blatted, a refugee who had been driven from place to place and tortured in all of them until he finally reached London, couldn't stand it any more. He cut his throat and jumped out of a high window. A girl, who was driving an ambulance that night, says, 'I remember how angry I was with him. I understand it a little now, but that night I was furious with him. There were so many who got it that night and they couldn't help it. I shouted at him I hoped he would die, and he did.'

'People save such strange things. One elderly man lost his whole house by fire. He saved an old rocking chair. He took it everywhere with him; wouldn't leave it for a moment. His whole family was killed, but he hung on to that rocking chair. He wouldn't sit in it. He sat on the ground beside it, but you couldn't get it away from him.'

Two reporters sat out the blitz in the Savoy Hotel, playing chess and *fortifying themselves*. When the bombs came near they went under the table. 'One or the other of us always reached up and cheated a little,' the reporter says.

Hundreds of stories and all of them end with a little incident, a little simple thing that stays in your mind.

'I remember the eyes of people going to work in the morning,' a man says. 'There was a quality of tiredness in those eyes I haven't forgotten. It was beyond a tiredness you can imagine–a desperate kind of weariness that never expected to be rested. The eyes of the people seemed to be deep, deep in their heads, and their voices seemed to come from a long distance. And I remember during a raid seeing a blind man standing on the curb, tapping with his stick and waiting for someone to take him across through the traffic. There wasn't any traffic, and the air was full of fire, but he stood there and tapped until someone came along and took him to a shelter.'

In all of the little stories it is the ordinary, the common-place thing or incident against the background of the bombing that leaves the *indelible picture*.

- What important points do you think the author was trying to get across in this description?
- Here is a list of statements. Each one is linked to something the author has written. However, some of the statements summarize important main points the author is making; others refer to less important matters.
- Put the statements in your own order of importance. Start by choosing the one that comes closest to what the passage is about. Then move down to less important points.
- When you have done this, compare your answers with a partner, and discuss your differences.

  a) During the blitz there were deafening sounds of bombs screaming and exploding, and the air was full of fire.
  b) Londoners are full of amusing and fascinating stories about life during the air raids.
  c) The most memorable thing about people during the blitz was the desperate tiredness in their eyes.
  d) People who have had frightening experiences are often helped by sharing their stories with others.
  e) The strain of living under constant bombardment caused many people to behave irrationally–to do things they would not normally have done.
  f) Most people who recollect the bombing are haunted by memories of trivial but vivid details.
  g) The stress of danger from fire and explosion drove a lot of people to suicide.
  h) People, birds and animals and even trees were destroyed on a horrifying scale during the London bombings.
  i) The danger of losing their property made some people very selfish and possessive about the things they owned.
  j) Blind people were particularly endangered during the horror of the blitz.

- Now answer these questions:

  a) Say what you think the words and phrases in italic mean as used in the passage:
     i) invariably
     ii) comprehensible
     iii) fortifying themselves
     iv) indelible picture

b) Imagine that you were alive during the blitz. What details do you think would stick in your mind? Which items of personal property would you most fear losing? Write a short but vivid account, starting 'I shall never forget one particular night . . . '.

Answers on page 109

C A visit to Jamaica

In this piece of writing, Marcia, a young student, describes part of a visit she made to Jamaica where her parents were born.

After one week I went to stay with another family of cousins in a little country area by the name of Mores which is not too far from Maypen. It was a beautiful place with beautiful people. Everyone living in the area was related somehow or other. I liked this because it gave the place a close family feeling and a sense of belonging. My sister and myself were to stay there for one week while my mum, granny and brother went off visiting. I was glad about this because then I wouldn't have my mother hanging around me, telling me what to do and what not to do. I would get up in the mornings and head straight down to the river for a wash. Everybody who lived in the country parts went to the river to wash. Boys and girls, old and young would bathe in the river, taking off all their clothes and not worrying who the hell was watching them.

I remember the first time I went to the river and saw a young girl around the age of eighteen bathing naked. I didn't know where to put my face. I didn't know whether I should look at her or turn my face away. Eventually when I did turn my face away, I saw all these young boys diving naked from high rocks and seeing this I just couldn't turn my face away from them, not frightened of what I saw but surprised that they just couldn't care two hoots.

In the morning, afternoon and nights I would always receive fruit from friends and family who I had met there. I would have bananas, mangoes, sugar cane, guavas and all the fruits they could get hold of. The house in which I was staying had orange trees, mango trees and sugar cane just outside so if I was thirsty I would just walk a few steps and then pick an orange off the trees.

Friends would come to the house and ask me if I were going to the river. We'd bring fruits and cook our own food down there. We would spend the whole day there until it was nearly dark, then go on our way home. I can still remember how the river water looked. It was unforgettable! It was clear; you could see right through it. It was good drinking water which people would come to fetch regularly.

Coming from the river we would usually get dressed, about thirty of us, and go to the main attraction of Clarendon, which was Maypen. We would buy hot corn on the cob from the people who would sell them on the roadsides and sometimes fried chicken and rolls with sodas. Coming home around three o'clock in the morning we would then go off to our own homes. We would do the same thing all over again the next day. The Jamaicans I met seemed to be very easy-going people. They would do things that the English would not ever dream of doing, for instance staying out very late at night.

The school children I saw in Jamaica were extremely tidy. Their uniforms which they had to wear, were always very neatly pressed, and their shoes had to be well shined. The hair was always neat and clean. The students looked as tidy coming home from school as when they went.

Jamaican parents are also very strict towards their children, not all of them but most of them. When I was there I wore lipstick and a bit more make-up than usual. When one of my aunties noticed she began to tell me off and asked if I thought I was a woman or something. I suppose this was a reflection of her strong religious attitudes. I explained that our way of living in Britain is completely different and told her that if a girl of fifteen and upwards were to wear make-up in England no one would really say anything, and it is actually quite common for a girl of that age to wear it.

A lot of young girls in Jamaica have babies very early, from the age of thirteen upwards. A few boys asked me if I weren't going to have one and were quite surprised really when I answered, 'no'. One or two of them even went to the extreme of asking me if they could 'breed' me so that they could be the father of my baby. I thought it quite strange that they were not allowed to wear make-up, but when it came to getting pregnant, which is a more serious matter, it was not looked upon so seriously.

Meetings were held for the younger generation to discuss what they thought needed to be done in their parish. The parish councillor would be called in once a month to discuss their problems with them. He would then see if he could help them in any way. These meetings would take place two or three nights a week and would start at around six or seven. I thought this was a very good idea because it gave the younger girls and boys a chance to have a say in what was to be done in their town. It is usually the older generation who have their say in everything and here the youth learn to participate in the running of their country and parishes early.

A very important aspect of the Jamaican's life is music. Everywhere I went in the country, reggae music could be heard. This music originates from Jamaica and it is one thing they can hold on to and nobody, but nobody can take this away from them. The music comes out of the shanty town in Kingston and is a product of the Rasta culture.

- Some of these statements about the extract are true; some are false. Sort out which are which, and compare your answers with a partner.

  a) Reggae music started in Kingston, Jamaica.
  b) People in Mores could not use river water to drink because the whole community washed and bathed in it.
  c) Marcia felt rather lonely at first without her mother, granny and brother around.
  d) Jamaica is plentiful in fruit and vegetation.
  e) Religion is an important part of Jamaican life.
  f) One of the pleasant things about school in Jamaica is that you don't have to wear uniform.
  g) There is little real poverty in Jamaica.
  h) Marcia found everything about the Jamaican way of life superior to that in Britain.

- Now answer these questions:

  a) Marcia says 'There are a lot of contradictions in Jamaica'. Find three pieces of evidence in the extract which support her view.

  b) It is clear that Marcia is a very effective writer, and her account makes vivid reading. However, there may be a few places where you would have expressed Marcia's ideas a little differently.

     With a partner decide on three sentences which you feel you would have expressed differently. Each of you write them out in your own style and discuss the changes you have made. Then decide which version you think is best.

  c) Using ideas from the passage, make a list of some of the differences a young person from Mores might find between her or his way of life and life in your own local community.

     Life in Mores, Jamaica Life in . . . , Britain

     When you have done this, try turning it into a description like Marcia's.

Answers on page 109

D Holiday insurance

The passage on page 60 is from a brochure about taking out insurance in case anything goes wrong on your holiday.

- Read it carefully and answer the questions.

a) The brochure was issued by the British Insurance Association. Is it an advertisement or is it simply giving you information? How do you know?

b) Name four things that can go wrong on holiday which a standard or *package policy* can insure you against.

c) How much does this insurance cost?

d) If you lose your luggage, what must you do in order to get the insurance money? Can you see any snags in this?

e) What is the usual amount you can claim if your holiday is cancelled?

f) What do the following phrases mean?
   i) *proof of notification*
   ii) *usual cover*
   iii) *holiday curtailment*
   iv) *personal liability*

g) How much do you get if you have an accident on holiday, e.g. loss of an eye?

h) What doesn't this pamphlet tell you that you might want to know if you were thinking of holiday insurance?

i) Did you find it easy to read?
Rewrite one of the sections, making it easier for people to understand.
e.g. *Medical Expenses*
'If you get ill or hurt on holiday . . .'

j) Having read this brochure would you take out holiday insurance? If so why, if not why not?

Answers on page 109

Why do I need Holiday Insurance

Whether you travel abroad or at home you run certain risks. You might fall ill or have an accident and need medical treatment; you could have your luggage stolen; you might injure someone, or damage their property and have to pay costs; or your holiday could be cancelled or cut short through accident or sickness. All these risks and more (see below) can be met by a holiday insurance package policy or by a selective holiday policy.

WHAT DOES A HOLIDAY POLICY COVER?

A **standard or package policy** usually covers the following:–

Luggage or articles worn or carried which are lost or damaged on holiday. Losses must be reported to the police within 24 hours and proof of notification obtained.
Usual cover **£500** or **£600.**

This usually includes a limit of £100 for lost money and there is usually a single article limit of £100 or £150.

Cancellation, where holiday costs are not recoverable, caused by accident, illness, quarantine, pregnancy (unknown when policy taken out) jury service or witness call. This section usually refers to you, close members of your family or business associates travelling with you or remaining at home. Holiday curtailment cover may also be included.

Some policies will also pay compensation if your departure is delayed beyond a specified period as a direct result of strike or industrial action.
Usual cover **£300–£600**

Medical Expenses including cover for additional hotel and travel expenses related to sickness or injury and expenses incurred in returning home due to injury, illness or death of a friend, relative or business associate travelling with you. The first few pounds of any claim are usually excluded.
Usual cover **£5000 upwards**

Note–For North America, medical expenses cover under a package policy may not be sufficient, and you are strongly advised to consult your insurance company, broker or travel agent about any necessary additional cover.

Personal Accident benefits on death or permanent disablement or loss of an eye or limb
Usual cover **£2000** or **£2500**
Temporary disablement **Weekly benefits**

Personal Liability covers your legal liability for injury or damage you cause to others and their property
Usual cover **£250,000**
Note–Some policies cover you only for awards made in UK courts.

How much does it cost?

Normally about £8 per adult (sometimes less for children) for a fortnight's cover in Europe and the Mediterranean area although premiums are usually higher for the USA and Canada. Some standard of package travel policies can be purchased in units and if the sums insured for one unit are not sufficient you can double them by taking out an additional unit.

You can if you wish buy a selective policy which enables you to obtain insurance for longer periods than under a package policy and to buy increased sums insured for some risks and ignore others.

E Keeping fit–past and present

What kind of advice did people get about keeping fit a hundred and fifty years ago? How does this advice compare with the kind we receive today?

- The two extracts which follow are about the physical benefits of walking and jogging. Read them both through carefully, then see how much they both have in common by answering the questions on page 64.

IMPROVING HEALTH AND PROLONGING LIFE
by A. Physician (1827)

Walking There is no exercise so natural to us, or in every respect so conducive to health, as walking. It is the most perfect in which the human body can be employed; for by it every limb is put in motion, and the circulation of the blood is effectually carried on, throughout the minutest veins and arteries of the system. Both the body and the mind are enlivened by walking; and even when carried to an extreme, it has often been found highly serviceable in nervous diseases. This salutary and most excellent exercise is in the power of every body having the use of their limbs, and can be adapted, in degree and duration, to the various circumstances and wishes of each individual.

Walking is of two kinds, either on plain ground, or where there are ascents. The latter is in every respect greatly preferable, as by it the lungs are exercised, and the ascent and descent agitates the body, unless it be in a weak state, with a useful variety. Walking against a high wind is very severe exercise, and not to be recommended.

It was an old rule, *'after dinner to set a while, and after supper to walk a mile;'* but that adage is not consistent with the hours kept in modern times. When supper, however, was very early, those who resided in the country might have the advantage of walking two or three miles previous to their going to bed. It is said that such a walk brought on a gentle breathing sweat, which was favourable to repose; and that next morning, they awoke with a clear head, and found refreshment from their sleep, of which the indolent have no idea.

The following rules are recommended to the attention of those who are attached to this excellent species of exercise. 1 The most proper walk, for health, is in a pure and dry air, and in rather an elevated situation, avoiding marshy and damp plains. 2 In the summer season, the walk to be taken morning and evening, but by no means during the middle of the day, unless guarded from the oppressive heat of the sun, under the shade of woods or forests; in winter, the best period of the day is usually after breakfast, or from ten to one. 3 It is advisable, occasionally to change the place where you walk, for the same place, constantly gone over, may excite as many disagreeable and painful sensations as the closet or the study. 4 We ought to accustom ourselves to a steady and regular, but not to a very quick pace; in setting out, it should be rather slower than what we afterwards indulge in. 5 An agreeable companion contributes much to serenity of mind; but unless the mode of walk is similar, as well as the taste and character congenial, it is better to walk alone; as either one or the other of the two companions must be subjected to some constraint. 6 To read during a walk is an improper action, highly detrimental to the eyes, and destroys almost all the good effects that can be derived from the exercise.

The celebrated Captain Barclay's *style of walking* is to bend forward the body, and to throw its weight on the knees. His step is short, and his feet are raised only a few inches from the ground. Any person who will try this plan, will find that his pace will be quickened, at the same time he will walk with more ease to himself, and be better able to endure the fatigue of a long journey, than by walking in a position perfectly erect, which throws too much of the weight of the body on the ankle-joints. He always uses thick-soled shoes, and lamb's wool stockings. It is a good rule to shift the stockings frequently during the performance of a long distance; but it is indispensably requisite to have shoes with thick soles, and so large, that all unnecessary pressure on the feet may be avoided.

THE GENTLE JOG TO FITNESS

Jogging not only makes you feel great, it is also one of the most natural and effective ways of exercising the heart and lungs. Jogging is running free and easy, at a comfortable trot. There's no urgency, no strain, no competition.

The idea is to jog along at a pace that makes you no more than moderately breathless. If you do it for long enough and often enough, in gradually increasing sessions it will soon build up the stamina of your heart and lungs, and strengthen your leg muscles. And the steady, easy rhythm of jogging will help to massage away mental and physical tension and lift depression. The joy of jogging is that virtually anyone can do it, young or old. You can do it, anywhere or anytime.

How often?
As with any other heart and lung exercise, you will get most benefit if you jog as often as possible, preferably every day. But if you can't manage that, every other day is often enough. Less often and you lose the training effect.

How much depends entirely on your state of fitness. The most important thing is to build up your jogging very gradually week by week. This gives your heart, lungs and circulation time to develop the necessary stamina.

When?
The best time of day to jog is when it suits you. Maybe before breakfast when the air is fresh and the streets are quieter. Or perhaps in the early evening before supper, under cover of darkness. It depends on how you feel, and how your day is planned. But there are times when you should NOT jog:

* Don't jog within two hours of your last meal.
* Don't jog if you feel tired, weak or flaked-out.
* Don't jog if you have a cold or feel one coming on.
* Don't jog in fog.

Remember if you jog in the dark, always wear light-coloured kit so that you can be easily seen by fast moving traffic. Even better, wear a reflective jacket (obtainable from cycle shops).

How to start
Gently does it–especially if you are over 35, unfit, overweight or a smoker. Here's how to build up your effort gradually, little by little, day by day. You should always be well within your capability. If you feel flaked out, you've definitely overdone it.

Where?
Virtually wherever you like. But preferably away from diesel exhaust fumes. If you prefer to jog on soft ground, try the park or a country path or bridleway. Or get permission to use the local school playing field or local authority sports ground. Don't be tempted to sprint downhill during the first few weeks when it is more likely to cause muscle strain.

Jogging in company
Try jogging with a friend. It helps to pass the time. You could make it a family affair. Or perhaps join one of the hundreds of jogging clubs and groups that have blossomed up and down the country. Some of these are informal groups of friends, neighbours or workmates. Others are organized by local health and recreation authorities and sports centres.

Joggers' togs
Make yourself comfortable. As we've said, it depends a bit on the weather, but try to wear loose-fitting lightweight clothing. Natural fibre (such as cotton)

is much better than nylon or terylene. You won't get so hot and sticky. If you're too hot you'll exhaust yourself in no time. If you're too cold you may stiffen and get cramp. So wear a warm top that you can take off and sling round your waist when you start to warm-up. A track-suit is tailor-made for the job. And in cold weather keep your head warm with a hat or scarf.

The right footing

It is vital to wear the proper foot-gear. If you have an old pair of gymshoes that are well broken-in but haven't broken up, use them. If you're buying a new pair, watch out for the following points:

* Choose ones with a thick cushioned rubber insole, especially at the heel. This is important because it prevents jarring.
* Beware protruding stitches on the inside which might give you blisters.
* Avoid shoes with plastic linings that don't let your feet 'breathe'. Avoid shoes with high tabs at the back which can cut into your heel.
* Choose a shoe with a good arch support.
* You may need a size larger than your street shoes, if you wear thicker socks, as your feet may 'spread' a little when you jog.
* Break in new shoes by wearing them about the house for a few days before jogging in them.

a) The first twenty-four lines or so of each extract deal with the advantages of walking/jogging as forms of exercise. List three advantages they both agree on.

b) Do the writers agree about the best times of day for taking exercise? What differences are there?

c) The writers seem to take a different emphasis when discussing the best places for walking. Why might this be?

d) What is their advice on the matter of speed and pace of walking/jogging?

e) Do both writers agree that it is best to have company?

f) Name two things the writers both recommend about footwear.

g) Find two things which the modern writer has had to include in his advice which the earlier one had no need to.

h) In the first extract a number of words are used differently from the way they might be today. What words might you use to replace those which are in italic?

i) Walking is of two kinds, either on *plain* ground, or where there are ascents.
ii) the circulation of the blood is *effectually* carried on
iii) 'after dinner to *set* a while, and after supper to walk a mile'
iv) as many disagreeable and painful sensations as the *closet* or the study.

i) Which words or phrases in the modern extract might cause similar problems to readers in another hundred years or so?

Answers on page 110

6 Think again

Information

All the passages in this part of the book offer a different challenge to your skill in reading.

With some you have to gather information. With others you have to decide which version of events is nearer the truth. With yet others the main thing is to express your opinions. The basic point behind all of them is, however, the same, whatever the particular task. You have to be alert, questioning and accurate in your reading. In fact, you have to be a good reader.

A Cowboys and cattle herds

The next two extracts contain among other things a lot of information about controlling a cattle herd on a long drive. You are probably familiar with some of the basic facts about cattle driving because cattle scenes are often featured in epic westerns.

- Read the two passages carefully noting the important details.
- Then draw a diagram showing exactly what a cattle drive would have looked like and where the different people involved would be positioned.
- You need to include the following:

  chuck wagon, trail hands, remuda, straw boss, trail boss, cook, drag, flank, swing, point, wrangler, trail herd, mules

- Although in some cases you will not be able to draw each item individually, indicate the numbers of men and animals involved as well as where they would travel on the drive.
- When you have finished compare your diagram with a partner and discuss whose is the more accurate. You will probably need to read the extracts again to do this.

CONTROLLING A CATTLE HERD ON A LONG DRIVE

The recollections of Charles Goodnight

When I made up my mind that I was going to drive, I set about collecting my outfit. My first step was to round up fifty or sixty good horses. Then the mess wagon (chuck wagon) was made ready with provisions. Meantime I informed my neighbour stockman that I was to drive to a northern market and would receive any cattle they wanted to go with the herd, arranging for the concentration of the herd at some given point, where the cattle were branded with a trail brand. I was never over three days in putting the average herd of three thousand head together.

Our outfit consisted of sixteen to eighteen men, a mess wagon drawn by four mules, driven by the cook, and a horse wrangler who had charge of the horse herd (remuda). These men were thoroughly drilled regarding their places and duties. I always selected two of the most skilled to be my pointers, to handle the front of the herd and keep it on the course given out by the foreman (trail boss). I always selected three steady men for the rear to look out for the weaker cattle–the drags. The rest of the men were divided along the sides–the swing.

Trail hands were well disciplined and were governed entirely by signals, being too far from the leader to receive orders in any other way. The signals were mostly derived from the Plains Indians. They were all made from horseback, by movements of the hat.

The signal to break camp and move upon the trail, simply a motion with the hat in the direction to be followed, was repeated by the pointers and passed along to the rear. About eleven o'clock the signal to graze was passed along the line. Then the men ate dinner, which was prepared while breakfast was cooking. When the cattle began to lie down, the trail boss knew that they had grazed long enough, and gave the signal to resume the trail.

Extracts from Jim Herron's description of his first long drive up the Texas trail in 1880

I had always wanted to be a real cowboy. The 'Western Trail' passed close to the range where we held father's cattle. Many big herds passed that way daily in the summer months. One day a herd came swimming into sight. I learned that this herd was heading for the Black Hills in Dakota. I asked what the Boss's name was. They told me: 'Quinlan'. When I rode up I asked, 'You need a good man?' The boss stood up high in his stirrups and shaded his eyes with one hand, all the while looking across the prairie. 'Wheah is this man?' he asked, 'I sho don't see him.' The two men with him howled with laughter.

I was assigned eight horses from the remuda, just like the other men had, for we changed two or three times each day. I was the proudest boy in Texas.

We headed north the next morning, me riding the drag. This was the worst job with the trail herd because of the thick dust. . . .

Everything went well until we reached the Wichita River. That morning Quinlan rode on ahead, as was his practice. We didn't think much of his failure to return until we saw his horse coming back later, dripping wet and lame. Pearl, the straw boss (deputy foreman) called the herd off the trail and told us to water them until he found Quinlan. We were at the river crossing for two days while they searched for Quinlan. Then they found Quinlan's body. It was washed up on a sandbar three miles down the stream. But we never learned how or why he drowned. We dug a grave on a little knoll a hundred yards south from the river, and there we buried our boss. The lesson I learned from his sad fate was that even a growed man could lose his life on the trail.

B The fight

The next extract contains various accounts of a fight which took place outside a school. The first is by an old lady who was walking along the road at the time; the next is by a window cleaner; the next by the headmaster of the school concerned; the next by a pupil involved in a fight and the last a report broadcast by a local radio station.

➔

- Read them through and as you read jot down notes of any differences you notice between the accounts.

  (It is best to read all the accounts through *quickly* and then re-read each version more carefully in order to make your notes.)

Old lady

I was walking home and I just got opposite the school–Devenport Comprehensive–you know it. Anyway, I was practically pushed into the traffic by this crowd of teenage thugs milling about, swearing–I think the language of these kids today is dreadful. One of them was shoving another one in the chest and yelling at him–something about a girl. The others were all egging them on. One of them was actually waving a penknife around. It's a wonder nobody was hurt. Luckily the police arrived in a van and started breaking it up. I know what I'd do to them if I was in charge. What they need is a good hiding. I think the police have a very hard job these days coping with that sort of thing. Still, they soon pushed them along and got rid of them.

Window cleaner–on the opposite side of the street
I didn't see much–just the usual group of kids all trying to push on to the bus. Seemed a bit more rowdy than usual, though. I think one of them was from another school–had a different uniform anyway. He was looking for a fight–all mouthy. You know how kids are. The girls are just as bad–yelling their heads off. One of them was crying and shrieking, hysterical. The funny part was the way some old dear laid into them with her handbag. Anyway, the police roared up, late as usual in a white Rover. It was all over by then, really.

Headmaster
This is most unfortunate. One of our pupils was involved in an altercation with a lad from another school. It was connected with a dispute about a girlfriend. I am proud of my school and am sure this incident was exceptional. Many of our senior pupils are involved in community work and we enjoy a good reputation in the area. The notion that people are terrorized by our pupils is a gross exaggeration. I dealt with the boy the following morning. I talked it over with him and have imposed a week's detention plus the loss of certain privileges. His parents have been contacted and agree with me that the matter should now be forgotten. I have no idea who called the police. Certainly no member of my staff would overreact in such a way.

Tracy
It was all Wayne's fault. He goes to St Jacobs round the corner. Anyway I gave him up two weeks ago and he's been going about threatening my current boyfriend. He was waiting outside the school and he called me a name and I got annoyed. He's a loud-mouthed bully–he is always involved in some aggro or other, him and his mates. My boyfriend gave him a mouthful and they had a go at each other. I could have killed him. All I had on me was a metal comb but I had a few jabs at him. I don't know what the fuss is all about. There's often a bit of bullying and fighting outside the school. The police pushed everybody about and we all went home.

Local radio news item
And now a disturbing report from one of the town's largest comprehensive schools–Devenport. Several pupils and members of the public were injured in an incident outside the school in Sidmouth Street. We go over now to our reporter on the scene . . .

Only a few hours ago this whole area was the scene of one of the most violent clashes we have seen in recent years involving pupils at the strife-torn Devenport Comprehensive. Members of staff refused to comment but Mr John Hurtson, the headmaster, issued a statement in which he claimed that 'the incident was exceptional' and that the pupils would be 'talked to' and 'the parents contacted'. Mr Hurtson maintained he was 'proud of the school', a view not shared by an elderly lady who was physically assaulted in the incident, which apparently involved a row over a fifth former's girlfriend. A local resident, Mrs Avely, saw a crowd of teenage thugs milling about and swearing. What made the fight particularly grave was the evidence of the weapons used. 'One of them was waving a penknife . . . it's a wonder nobody was hurt.' Another witness stated that 'the girls were just as bad–yelling their heads of . . . shrieking and hysterical'.

Luckily on this occasion the police arrived promptly and were able to subdue the crowd and limit the damage. One of the pupils of the school said a group of fifth years were 'always involved in some aggro or other'. She stated that there was 'often . . . bullying and fighting outside the school'.

Police are pursuing their enquiries but as yet no arrests have been made. In the meantime, local residents are asking is this what we must learn to expect from today's young people?

a) Now, with your notes in front of you, draw a diagram, sorting out the *facts* of what happened from people's *opinions*. Set it out like this:

WITNESS	FACTS	OPINIONS
Old Lady		
Window cleaner		
Headmaster		
(*etc.*)		

b) Write a newspaper report, including headlines, using the material you have just read. (Remember you will have to select those elements of the story which you think are most important and will sell your newspaper.) Like all the witnesses, you will have a particular point of view about the fight. How will this affect your treatment of the story?

c) Write Wayne's version of the fight. (You could if you prefer write the account of one of the other fifth years involved.)

d) *Either* write down the conversation between Tracy's boyfriend and the headmaster *or* say what you would do about fighting if you were headmaster of the school.

e) Write an account of a similar incident in which you yourself were involved.

C An unlikely story

One day Ian Nicol, a riveter by trade, started to split in two down the middle. The process began as a bald patch on the back of his head. For a week he kept smearing it with hair restorer, yet it grew bigger, and the surface became curiously puckered and so unpleasant to look upon that at last he went to his doctor. 'What is it?' he asked.
'I don't know,' said the doctor, 'but it looks like a face, ha, ha! How do you feel these days?'
'Fine. Sometimes I get a stabbing pain in my chest and stomach but only in the morning.'
'Eating well?'
'Enough for two men.'
The doctor thumped him all over with a stethoscope and said, 'I'm going to have you *X-rayed.* And I may need to call in a specialist.'

Over the next three weeks the bald patch grew bigger still and the suggestion of a face more clearly marked on it. Ian visited his doctor and found a specialist in the consulting room, examining X-ray plates against the light. 'No doubt about it, Nicol,' said the specialist, 'you are splitting in two down the middle.'
Ian considered this.
'That's not usual, it it?' he asked.
'Oh, it happens more than you would suppose. Among bacteria and viruses it's very common, though it's certainly less frequent among riveters. I suggest you go into hospital where the process can complete itself without annoyance for your wife or embarrassment to yourself. Think it over.'

Ian thought it over and went into hospital where he was put into a small ward and given a nurse to attend him, for the specialist was interested in the case. As the division proceeded more specialists were called in to see what was happening. At first Ian ate and drank with a greed that appalled those who saw it. After consuming three times his normal bulk for three days on end he fell into a coma which lasted till the split was complete. Gradually the lobes of his brain separated and a bone shutter formed between them. The face on the back of his head grew eyelashes and a jaw. What seemed at first a cancer of the heart became another heart. Convulsively the spine doubled itself. In a puzzled way the specialists charted the stages of the process and discussed the cause. A German consultant said that life was freeing itself from the vicissitudes of sexual reproduction. A psychiatrist said it was a form of schizophrenia, a psycho-analyst that it was an ordinary twinning process which had been delayed by a severe case of prenatal sibling rivalry. When the split was complete, two thin Ian Nicols lay together on the bed.

The resentment each felt for the other had not been foreseen or guarded against. In bed the original Ian Nicol could be recognized by his position (he lay on the right of the bed), but as soon as both men were strong enough to walk each claimed ownership of birth certificate, union card, clothes, wife and National Insurance benefit. One day in the hospital grounds they started fighting. They were evenly matched and there are conflicting opinions about who won. On leaving hospital they took legal action against each other for theft of identity. The case was resolved by a medical examination which showed that one of them had no navel.

The second Ian Nicol changed his name by deed poll and is now called Macbeth. Sometimes he and Ian Nicol write to each other. The latest news is that each has a bald patch on the back of his head.

a) Here are some possible titles for the story. Put them in the order you think suits it best.

   Divide and Rule
   The Spread of Ian Nicol
   Ian's Unusual Illness
   Splitting Images
   A Rivetting Tale

b) What is the first sign of Ian's problem?
c) What clues in his first interview with the doctor hint at what might happen?
d) Which of these statements best summarizes the attitudes of the doctor and specialist?

   They are greatly amused
   They are off-hand and unsympathetic
   They are reassuringly matter-of-fact
   They are totally confused

e) Discuss with a friend the different interpretations of the case made by the German consultant, the psychiatrist and the psychoanalyst. You may need to use a dictionary!
   Then write down what each of them may have meant using everyday language.
f) What hint does the last sentence of the story give as to what might happen next?

g) In some ways each of us is more than one person. Draw up a list of some of your own qualities under these two headings

The person I like and admire
The person I loathe and detest.

Write descriptions of each of these sides of yourself.
Like Ian, you might like to give your 'other half' a different name.

Answers on page 111

D Accident

- Read the following account of a traffic accident and study the diagram carefully.

At 7.55 am on 27 June an accident took place at the junction of Howard Road and Sawyer's Lane. A van and a car were involved, both of which were damaged. Traffic conditions were good. It was a bright sunny morning, the road was dry and visibility good. The driver of the van received facial injuries and broke his nose. The driver of the car was uninjured.

At first it seemed there were no witnesses to the accident, though later the driver of the car mentioned on his insurance report a man who said he had seen the accident as he was putting his dustbin out ready for the dustmen who were coming that day.

Both cars could be driven after the accident. The police were not called by either of the drivers but each one completed a statement to his insurance company describing the accident.

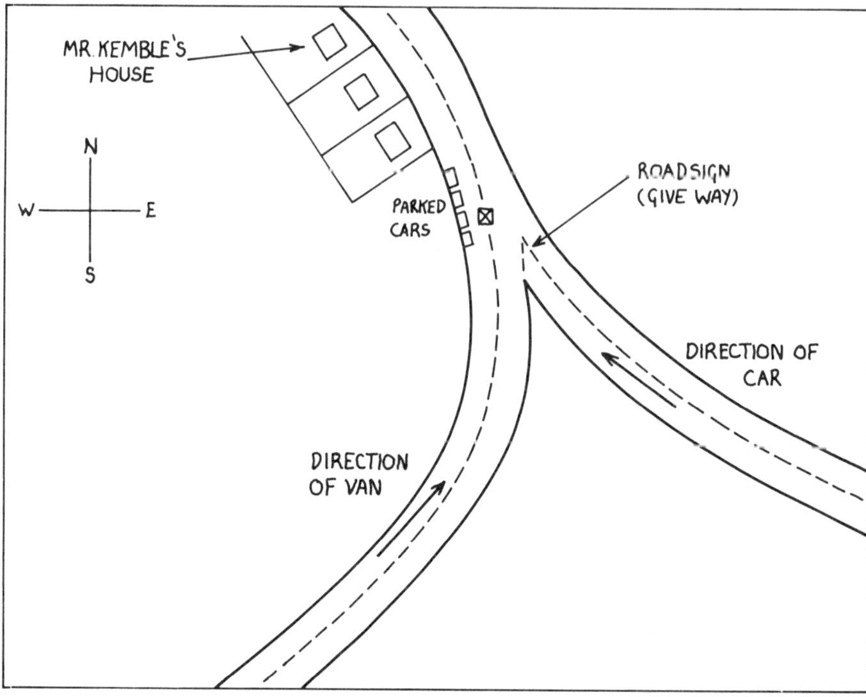

- Now read the drivers' statements carefully and note the details given about each driver's damage report on the vehicles, and the witness's statement.

Insurance statements

Car driver: Mr K. S. Tyrone aged 29

One endorsement for speeding. One previous insurance claim four years ago. Occupation: advertising executive. Ten years' driving experience. Owned car for three weeks.

Mr Tyrone's statement

I slowed down as I approached the junction of Sawyer's Lane and Howard Road. Coming to a halt, I naturally looked both ways up and down Howard Road. The junction is a tricky one because of the parked cars and on that morning it was doubly difficult because of the bright sunlight, shining directly into my eyes. Having made certain nothing was coming I carefully inched out. I was almost half way across Howard Road when a van, travelling I would guess at about 50 mph, suddenly came round the corner of Howard Road. He swerved to avoid a line of parked cars and he hit me at the point marked X on the diagram. I was almost stationary at the moment of impact.

Damage report
Car: B. M. W. 3202 (automatic) X registration

Left headlight smashed. Left indicator smashed. Front of left wing buckled. Tyre damaged. Steering geometry impaired. Battery (left-hand side under bonnet) cracked. No other damage.

Mr Kemble–a witness

I was putting my dustbin out when I heard a crash and saw Mr Tyrone's car and a van hitting each other. I knew that baker's van would be in trouble one day. He is always speeding past here in the mornings. I'm sure Mr Tyrone stopped at the junction because he knows it is a tricky one and a number of accidents have happened there.

Van driver: Mr T. M. Benson aged 47

Disqualified for one year nineteen years ago for drunken driving. Four previous insurance claims, the last one two years ago. Occupation: delivery driver for bakery firm. Twenty-five years' driving experience. The van was owned by Softa Bakery Co. Ltd.

Mr Benson's statement

I was travelling at about 29 mph up Howard Road on my morning delivery round. As I approached the junction of Sawyers Lane and Howard Road, I noticed a line of parked cars so I slowed down and indicated right and began to pull out to get round them. As I drew alongside Sawyers Lane a car rushed out of the turning and hit me at the point marked X on the diagram. I was sure he had not even slowed down at the junction. I was going to report him to the police but I was in a hurry to get my last delivery done and couldn't hang around all day. I didn't realize my nose was broken till some time later.

Damage report
Van: Leyland Sherpa R registration

Right-hand front door badly buckled. Right-hand door pillar out of alignment. Right floor still bent. Right wing to the rear of the door scratched and dented. Minor dents and scratching elsewhere obviously not connected with the accident.

The insurance companies involved exchanged statements and an assessor was asked to decide which company should pay for the damage.

- You are the assessor. Study the diagram, the facts and the statements and decide who is telling the truth and which, if any, driver was to blame. You may decide that no one was at fault in which case the insurance companies will share the repair costs equally. You may decide that each driver was partly to blame in which case you must state what proportion of the cost each should pay.
- Write a report, setting it out in the following way:

  'I considered the statement of Mr K. S. Tyrone, looked at the report on the damage to his car and have decided . . . .

  My opinion of the evidence of the witness Mr Kemble is . . . .

  I then examined Mr T. M. Benson's statement and the damage report on his car and I think . . . .

  My conclusion is that . . . .

  The costs of the accident should therefore be divided in the following way . . . .'

E Old folks

The following passage is taken from a newspaper article. In it a woman writes about a visit to her mother-in-law who is in an old people's home. Before reading the article discuss your own attitude to looking after old people when they become too frail to look after themselves.

- Consider the following questions.

  a) Should families of old people look after them?
  b) Do you feel you should be responsible for your own parents when they are old?
  c) Are old people's homes a solution to the problem of looking after old people?
  d) Can you make any suggestions of your own to help overcome the problem?

- Now read the newspaper article.

OLD FOLKS AT THE HOME

IT'S a modern unit, lying in a small hollow below the crest of the hill. As we approached in the car, my heart began its irregular thumping as the familiar symptoms of panic attacked me.

I told myself not to be so feeble; my husband looked calm and cheerful, and it must have been worse for him. After all, she's his mother.

We approached the locked swing doors. Glass they may be, but they're a kind of Iron Curtain, marking the end of the free world. Few of those behind them will ever emerge. Those who do will be under close escort and carefully returned.

We rang the bell. Some who will never learn came eagerly to the other side and pushed with eagerness at the unyielding door, until an orderly appeared, jangling keys.

The smell was not a hospital smell, but rather the smell of age and incontinence, ineffectually masked by disinfectants and air-fresheners. The whole unit was spotless, kept to its high standard by teams of scrubbing, scouring women.

We looked for Jack's mother, who keeps on the move, seldom settling in one place for more than 10 minutes. That day she was in the day-room, looking smart in her own green dress and cream cardigan, with her hair newly done.

We took her to the visitors' room, glancing in at the ward as we passed. Stainless orange coverlets gave the illusion of sunlight on a dull day.

Her bed was not always like these, clean, dry and inviting. I remembered an Easter Sunday, the day our growing suspicions of something horribly wrong hardened to certainty. Her house had become dusty and neglected. Often, sheets were festooned around her heater, filling the room with fetid steam. She would allow no one to enter her bedroom, and passing glimpses revealed only a neatly-made bed with a pretty cover.

But that day, with my husband to distract her attention, I managed to investigate beneath the orderly facade. I found layer upon layer of sodden blankets, and a urine-soaked mattress.

That afternoon, in her bedroom, I realized that the formidable, independent woman, who was my mother-in-law, now needed my help. She needed it, but would not want it. As I began to strip the bed, I heard her coming, protesting, enraged at this violation of her privacy.

Now, at least, she is warm and comfortable at night.

In the visitors' room we chatted brightly to her. She nodded and smiled at all we said, relaxed and mellow. She laughed a great deal, seeming happy and looked at me without rancour, even with liking.

Across the room, a woman wept helplessly to her wordless family. They glanced across longingly at our happy-looking group.

Things were not always so good between us. During the dark days, she cursed me with misery and hatred as I scraped her faeces off the carpet. And I, who should have known better, swore back at her.

A tea-trolley came rattling round. Tepid milky liquid was poured into saucer-less cups.

Beside the large aluminium teapot lay a sugar-encrusted spoon. At home, the spoon in our sugar-bowl is silver, topped with the figure of a golfer. Engraved on the back is the date, 1974, when she won it in the Medal Finals. We chatted to her about golf, reminding her of her achievements, but she laughed back at us, uncomprehending.

The tea did its work. Soon urine trickled down her legs, and she tensed, drawing in her breath. She was in pain from the raw patches caused by incontinence, which never completely heal. A nurse led her away to be changed.

I remembered when it was my job to change her. Our washing-machine went constantly during those months. The bed which had been changed at eight o'clock was wet again by noon, as she began to turn night into day. She never willingly accepted what she saw as interference on my part: why had she resented me so much, when now she went off chuckling with the nurse? Perhaps she had sensed that I, as much as she, shrank from the intimacy which had been forced upon us.

She returned freshly dressed, this time in a tired, ward-stock pinafore which scarcely reached her knees. She settled at the end of the ward. We kissed the soft, rosy face she raised, child-like, to us, and assured her of our return. She showed no inclination to come with us.

'It's so good she's happy,' said my husband. 'She seemed happy, don't you think?'

'Oh yes, very happy.'

We walked towards the car. I experienced the usual sense of relief, of having left behind some unbearable burden. We met a friend, who asked Jack about his mother.

'It's so sad,' she said. 'She was such a fine person. So bright and capable! Just the very last person on earth you'd ever think. . . .'

I remember further back, to the woman I first met 17 years ago. Tall and handsome, with a pretty complextion and vivid blue eyes, she treated me with unfussy friendliness. Her life was very full, with husband and friends and golf. I think we got on as well as most mothers and daughters-in-law, but I did not love her, nor did she expect it of me.

Perhaps I should feel guilty that I find I can love the gentle, smiling child she has become, but what I feel is gratitude.

I want to say to her, 'Thank you for being happy in this place. Thank you for not weeping, and begging to be let out. Thank you for preserving our peace of mind.'

- After you have read it make notes under the following headings. Put down as many points as you can under each heading.

  a) *The conditions in the old people's home*
  e.g. 1) The home was kept spotlessly clean.
  2) . . . .
  b) *How the old lady lived immediately before going into the home*
  e.g. 1) She didn't allow anyone to go into her bedroom.
  2) . . . .
  c) *What the old lady was like when she was younger*
  e.g. 1) She played a lot of golf
  2) . . . .
  d) *The writer's attitude to her mother-in-law*
  e.g. 1) She felt the symptoms of panic when she approached the home
  2) . . . .

- After you have done this, read the following poem. It was written by an old lady living in an old people's home. She was unable to speak although the nurses saw her writing from time to time. This poem was found in her locker after her death.

What do you see nurses
  what do you see?
Are you thinking
  when you are looking at me
A crabbit old woman,
  not very wise,
Uncertain of habit
  with far-away eyes,
Who dribbles her food
  and makes no reply,
When you say in a loud voice
  'I do wish you'd try'
Who seems not to notice
  the things that you do,
And forever is losing
  a stocking or shoe,

Who unresisting or not
  lets you do as you will
With bathing and feeding
  the long day to fill,
Is that what you're thinking,
  is that what you see?

Then open your eyes nurse,
  you are not looking at me,
I'll tell you who I am,
  as I sit here so still;
As I use at your bidding,
  as I eat at your will.

I'm a small child of ten
  with a Father and Mother,
Brothers and sisters who
  love one another,
A young girl of sixteen,
  with wings on her feet,
Dreaming that soon now
  a lover she'll meet:
A bride soon at twenty,
  my heart gives a leap,
Remembering the vows
  that I promised to keep:
At twenty-five now
  I have young of my own
Who need me to build
  a secure happy home.
A woman of thirty,
  My young now grow fast,
Bound to each other
  with ties that should last.
At forty my young sons
  now grown and will all be gone
But my man stays beside me
  to see I don't mourn.

At fifty once more
  babies play round my knee,

Again we know children
  my loved one and me.
Dark days are upon me,
  my husband is dead,
I look at the future
  I shudder with dread,
For my young are all busy
  rearing young of their own,
And I think of the years
  and the love I have known,
I'm an old woman now
  and nature is cruel,
'Tis her jest to make
  old age look like a fool.
The body it crumbles,
  grace and vigour depart,
There now is a stone
  where once I had a heart:
But inside this old carcase
  a young girl still swells.
And now and again
  my battered heart swells,
I remember the joys,
  I remember the pain,
And I'm loving and living
  life over again,
I think of the years
  all too few–gone too fast.
And accept the stark fact
  that nothing can last.

So open your eyes nurses,
  open and see,
Not a crabbit old woman,
  Look closer–see ME.

by Kate

- How has this poem and this article changed your attitude to old people and the whole problem of caring for them? Write a paragraph explaining your point of view clearly.

7 Make up your mind

A The case of the strange suicide

The next passage is taken from a detective story. In this type of story you often have to read very carefully so that you can pick up clues which the writer leaves for you to find. The trouble is, a good detective story writer doesn't make it easy for you to work out who the guilty person is. He puts in plenty of false and confusing details. In this extract, for example, there is one vital point which suggests that the chauffeur isn't telling the truth. Check through the exact description of what happened and also what the chauffeur says and answer the question,

'What made Inspector Bower suspicious of him?'

THE CASE OF THE STRANGE SUICIDE

Inspector Bower braked hard as he pulled up in front of the big office building. Ahead of him a patrol car sat, flashing its blue message. The white door stood open, an indication of how fast the driver had responded to the emergency call.

Bower pressed through the crowd that had gathered on the pavement. There is nothing to see, he said to himself, but crowds gather anyway. All you need to do is turn on your blue light, and you've got people all over the place. And they all want to see blood, too!

'They're up there!' a doorman was shouting at him.

'Who's up there?' Bower wanted to know.

'Your policeman and the man who turned on the alarm! He saw it all you know! He saw the man kill himself!' The doorman was very excited.

Bower looked around the lobby. 'Where's the lift?' he asked.

'It's broken!' the doorman said. 'You'll have to use the stairs. Fourth floor. The door's right over there.'

Inspector Bower was puffing by the time he made it up to the scene. The constable was standing in the doorway with a tall man in a chauffeur's uniform.

'This way, inspector!' said the constable. 'The body's still there. We haven't touched a thing.' He pointed to the chauffeur. 'This man is a witness. Saw the man hang himself.'

The office was big. And it was rich. The furniture was expensive, the rug was thick. There was a bar set into one wall. In fact, Bower thought, the only thing wrong was the body of a middle-aged man, a rope around his neck, hanging from the ceiling. Beneath him, an upturned footstool lay on the rug.

Bower walked over to the window, pulled the curtains and looked out. The crowd was still there and getting larger. Two more police cars had come in and added to the excitement. He turned to the chauffeur.

'You're the witness, eh? Do you know the dead man?'

'Well yes. He's–was–my boss! I was coming to pick him up. That's the limousine out in front. The grey one.'

Inspector Bower looked at him carefully. 'Tell us what happened.'

'Well, I just pulled in front and got out. The boss always limped a bit, see, and I was going to help him down the stairs. When I got out of the car, I looked up. I always do 'cause sometimes he waits on the balcony. He gets mad if I'm late. Anyway, I looked up, see, and there he was getting up on that footstool with the rope around his neck. And I know he's going to kill himself, see, but with the elevator broken, by the time I ran up four floors, he was dead already, see?'

'Yes I see,' said Bower. 'I think you'd better come with me. You've got more to tell us.'

B Murder in the park

The following mystery is loosely based on an actual murder, committed recently. The problem here is not simply to pick up an odd clue but to weigh evidence carefully and decide who the guilty person might be. (Remember: a jury must be satisfied 'beyond reasonable doubt' that someone is guilty.)

- Read the account of the murder carefully and then the statements of the witnesses.

MURDER IN THE PARK

In Pondsworth Park on the afternoon of 2 May, Fred Burgoyne was sitting in his hut drinking tea. I had been a hard day in the park. Springtime was the busiest time of the year for him. He had started work that day at 7.00 am and had only just finished at 5.30 pm. He had spent the day planting out the dahlias, geraniums and marigolds from the greenhouses. He still had to mow the bottom lawn, but at least he had been paid and was looking forward to a quiet drink in the pub before going home for tea. He enjoyed Fridays; it was the end of the working week and he could spend the weekend on his allotment. Secretly he liked the time when he was away from Doreen, his wife. They didn't really get on and he suspected she had been seeing a neighbour, Bill Jarvis, on the quiet. 'So what,' he thought, 'she can do what she likes for all I care.'

His thoughts were cut fatally short when an iron bar hit him on the back of the head, again and again until he lost consciousness. His week's wage, £72, was stolen.

Mrs Doreen Burgoyne was not really concerned when her husband failed to return home for his tea. She knew her husband liked to stop at the pub for a drink on Friday nights. Besides, she had her own life to live and she had plans for this weekend, while Fred was away on the allotment. If only Bill was not so jealous the set-up would be perfect. She and Fred had lived separate lives now for years, but she was quite comfortable in her home and she certainly wasn't going to divorce Fred as Bill Jarvis was always pressing her to do. His ranting and raving sometimes spoilt their times together.

It was not until 11.20 pm that evening that Doreen Burgoyne became alarmed and phoned the police, and at 7.30 am the following morning Fred Burgoyne's stretched-out body was discovered by Don Matthews, an apprentice park-keeper, when he had gone into the hut to make the morning tea. Later police investigation revealed that a disco had taken place in a hall on the far side of the park that evening and that many fans had used the park as a short cut.

Some had been rowdy and some damage had been done to flower beds and park benches on their route.

Police also discovered that Don Matthews had a record of petty crime including two convictions for shoplifting. He at first claimed that he had had the whole of Friday off and that he had spent the time at home planting roses in his garden.

His wife confirmed this. She also stated that two rough-looking men had called at eight o'clock that morning and that her husband had argued with them. She said he was 'frightened looking' and 'as white as a sheet'. Don Matthews himself admitted he owed various bookmakers over £500 in gambling debts and that the men had threatened him.

Later, after police had produced a witness who identified him, Matthews admitted he had gone to the park that Friday afternoon to see if he could borrow £20 from Fred Burgoyne. He wanted to use the money for a bet on a horse so that he could win back the money and pay off his debts. Burgoyne had refused but they had not quarrelled and Burgoyne was, according to Matthews, 'perfectly fit' when he left the hut.

Police appealed for witnesses and several came forward.

Witnesses

Mrs Skelton was walking her miniature poodle in the park at about 5.15 pm as she did every afternoon. She knew by sight both Burgoyne and Matthews. She had left her home and crossed the bottom lawn of the park, where she noticed a large motor mower left in the middle of the grass. She remembered feeling annoyed that council property, which she had paid her rates for, should be left outside overnight. As she walked on, she met Don Matthews, who she later identified, and was about to mention the mower, when he pushed past her on his bike without a word and rode off in the direction of the High Street exit of the park.

Mr Boothroyd was coming home from work and decided, as it was a nice evening, to walk through the park. As he entered the park from the High Street he was knocked down by a large unshaven man in a yellow shirt with dark stains down the front. He ran over the road and down a side street. Mr Boothroyd was not certain but he thought there might have been another man with the first about a hundred yards behind. He had been too busy picking himself up off the ground to notice. The time, he said, was between five and six o'clock.

The Rev Stanley Clifford came forward to testify that he had known Don Matthews for over thirteen years and had always found him hardworking and quiet with no indication that he could ever be capable of violence. Matthews had worked part-time as gardener at the rectory until he had got the job at the park.

Mr Bill Jarvis was interviewed when neighbours revealed to the police his affair with Doreen Burgoyne. He said he had been off sick with a cold on Friday and had spent most of the day in bed. In the afternoon he had got up and accompanied his wife to SuperFood Supermarket in the High Street to buy the weekend shopping. His wife confirmed this but staff at the supermarket did not remember seeing either of them.

Mrs Maureen Prestwick was pushing her pram through the park at about 5.30 pm after visiting her mother. She was in a hurry to get home. At the entrance to the park there was a crowd of noisy teenagers hanging about and getting in her way. As she passed she heard one of them ask what the hell they were going to do before the disco opened. Another had replied that they could 'have a laugh in the park'. When she saw the young park-keeper, later identified as Don Matthews, she though he would stop and tell the youngsters off, but he rode straight at them on his bike so they were forced off the path. She thought at the time that the park-keeper was setting a bad example, riding so fast.

a) Write down all the possible suspects in the case then use the following table to weigh up the evidence for and against each one.
(There are at least four suspects and possibly more)

Suspect	Motive	Opportunity	Alibi	Verdict	Reasons

b) On 14 October 1982 Don Matthews was charged with murder. Imagine you are members of the jury. You have the facts and the witnesses' statements. You have considered the evidence. What is your verdict? Do you find Matthews guilty or not guilty? If you cannot make up your mind on a verdict with only the evidence in front of you, write down extra questions you would like to ask any of the witnesses or other people involved in the case.

Set it out like this:

e.g. *Witness: Mrs Skelton*
1) 'Did you notice anybody following Don Matthews when he pushed past you on his bike?'

When you have done this for everybody you wish to interview, you might like to supply answers to your own questions (or get a partner to). Now you are in a better position to decide who is guilty.

What is your final verdict?

Decisions

In each of the next cases you have to make a decision based on a careful reading of the evidence before you. In real life, people's lives would be altered by decisions like the ones you will have to take so make sure you have good reasons for making up your mind in the way that you do.

C Parole board

All five of the following people qualify for parole, which means they can be let out of prison on condition that they do not commit another offence.

You are on the parole board, making that decision.

- Read the case notes of each one and make your own notes giving reasons for and against paroling them. When you have done that for each individual you have to decide which ONE should be released early. Write down clear reasons for your choice.

1 NAME:	TIMOTHY WANG SIN
AGE:	21 years
OFFENCE:	Demanding money with menace. Nothing previous
DATE OF CONVICTION AND SENTENCE	6.6.80 4 years
REMARKS:	Timothy arrived in Britain as an orphan from Vietnam in 1968. He appears to be half American and half Vietnamese. He has never been granted a British passport despite having lived in this country for as long as he can remember. When he is discharged from prison he is due for deportation from Britain. He has lived with a British girl for three years and they have a young daughter. He says he threatened a shopkeeper in order to get money to continue his studies. He admitted his offence and said he would not have harmed the shop-keeper. Parolled, he says he will continue his studies (in hotel management) and try to obtain a British passport and stay in the country.

2 NAME:	DOROTHY MALONE
AGE:	31 years
OFFENCE:	Fraud. Income tax evasion. Failing to keep proper company accounts. Starting a company while being an undischarged bankrupt. Passport offences.
DATE OF CONVICTION AND SENTENCE:	29.4.80 4 years
REMARKS:	Miss Malone is a university graduate, extremely able, particularly in the business field. She started a secretarial business which failed owing a lot of money. She blames this on partners. Since then she has been involved in numerous shady ventures, the last of which was a video-copying agency. She still maintains she was only going abroad on holiday when she was arrested at the airport for various currency offences. She is smart in appearance and would probably be able to find a job quite easily.

3 NAME	JAMES BERRY
AGE:	53 years
OFFENCE:	Various youthful offences, numerous breaking and entering. Receiving stolen property. Failure to pay maintenance to divorced wife. Numerous convictions for burglary once with violence. Numerous drunk and disorderly.
DATE OF CONVICTION AND SENTENCE	12.12.79 5 years
REMARKS:	James Berry has always been on the fringe of serious crime. He did not do well at school but is very intelligent and quite an expert on silver and antiques. He has a drink problem but prison staff say he has made considerable efforts to overcome it. He says his biggest mistake was 'marrying a woman who never stopped asking for money'. He would like to work in an antique shop but with his record this seems unlikely. His married daughter says she will put him up till he finds work. While in prison he studied for and obtained a certificate in librarianship. He is very convincing in interviews.

4 NAME:	JOHN BINFIELD
AGE:	24 years
OFFENCE:	Armed robbery. Conspiracy to rob. Several breaking and entering. Assaulting a police officer. Numerous petty offences.
DATE OF CONVICTION AND SENTENCE	17.12.78 10 years
REMARKS:	John Binfield was brought up in a variety of foster homes as he was deserted by his parents at an early age. His first offence–for shoplifting–was at the age of eight. Since then he has been in and out of prison. He is educationally sub-normal. The happiest period of his life was two years in a detention centre in the country where he learned to be a gardener and look after animals. He is easily influenced by others. Prison officers think he could go straight if he could get a job on a farm away from people to lead him into crime. He is unmarried.

5 NAME:	DAPHNE BROADHURST
AGE:	61 years
OFFENCE:	Murder.
DATE OF CONVICTION AND SENTENCE:	1.3.71
REMARKS:	Daphne Broadhurst murdered her mother in a fit of rage. She stabbed her repeatedly through the chest with a carving knife. Miss Broadhurst had looked after her mother for twenty-five years and for the last five of those years her mother was bedridden. Old Mrs Broadhurst was very difficult and dominant, and she treated her daughter as a child and a slave. At her trial the prosecution alleged that Miss Broadhurst stood to inherit her mother's money. As it turned out this sum was only a few hundred pounds. In prison Miss Broadhurst has been a model prisoner working quietly in the library. She has never shown any signs of violence. In recent years she has been suffering from arthritis.

D Job applications

In this next case you are an employer who has recently placed the advertisement on page 92 in the local newspaper.

You have received a number of applications for this job. You have selected the best four and have written or phoned to the candidates' schools for references.

In front of you are the best four candidate's letters of application and school reports.

JUNIOR
CLERICAL ASSISTANT

We are looking for a young person who has recently left school for employment in our Head Office in Greatcaster.

Work will commence in the accounts department, but a clerical career could mean involvement with our computer as well as telephone work and customer liaison.

If you are interested and have good examination results, please contact Mrs R. Jenkins, Personnel Officer, Timkins Products Limited, Astra House, Greatcaster, GT1

- From this written evidence place the candidates in order, with the person you think is best qualified to do the job first, your second choice next and so on. Write down the reasons you have placed each one in the particular order.
- Set it out like this:
  I think . . . is best suited to the job for the following reasons . . . .
  I think . . . should come next because . . . and so on.

  The candidates are:
  Pamela French Karen Walsh William Bartlett Silvia Morley

For this last candidate, you had to ring up the school for a reference as there wasn't time for a written one. You spoke to the Fifth Year Tutor, a Mr Rufus. This is what he said:

'Oh yes, Silvia Morley. Now let me see. I've got her records in front of me. She passed three 'O' levels in Art, English and Maths and four CSEs, French, Geography, History and Physics.

What was she like? . . . Nice girl. Plenty of energy. Always talking about some craze or other. I think she said she was going to travel when she left school. Didn't get very far if she's applying for a job in Greatcaster, did she? Attractive girl, all the boys liked her. On the other hand she did try to turn the old charm on when she hadn't done her homework–and it worked most of the time! I wouldn't have said she'd settle into office work very well, but she would get on fine with your customers. I think she's ambitious and she works harder than she lets on, especially when she's interested in something. You never know, maybe she's destined to be managing director of Timkins . . . .'

47 Placing Avenue
Wilmshurst
Greatcaster

Mrs R Jenkins,
Personnel officer,
Timkins Products Ltd,
Astra House,
Greatcaster
84B 9QS

1st October

Dear Mrs Jenkins

I am getting in touch with a view to applying for the post of Clerical Assistant at your firm. I have tried for a number of jobs since leaving school, so far without success. I think I can say without boasting that I am a hard worker. I am sure my old school will confirm this.

I have always wanted to do office work but unfortunately I was not able to do typing at school, though I am now going to evening classes in both shorthand and typewriting.

Wilmshurst is only half an hour's bus ride from Greatcaster so the job would be very convenient for me. I am available if you should want to interview me at any time, because, as I have already said, I have not yet found a job.

Yours sincerely,

Pamela French

St Stimlins School
Greatcaster
Wessex

Headmaster P.F. Woodhurst B.Ed

Mrs A. Jenkins
Personnel Officer,
Timkins Products Ltd.,
Astra House,
Greatcaster

8th October

Dear Mrs Jenkins,

Thank you for your enquiry concerning Pamela French.

Pam was a pupil at St Stimlins for the last two years of her schooling, having moved into the area when she was fourteen. I taught her myself and she proved an exceptionally diligent student, catching up quickly with work she had missed. She was an above-average student gaining 'O' levels in English (Grade B), French (D), History (C) and Home Economics (C) and CSE in Maths (Grade 3) and Biology (Grade 2).

Pamela is a capable and self-contained person; she tends to be over-critical of herself and is rather anxious and shy.

I believe she has taken on a large part of the responsibility of her younger sister and brother since the death of her mother eighteen months ago. Quite frankly I was amazed at how well she did in the exams considering her family difficulties.

Pamela is best with individuals or small groups rather than with crowds or strangers. On first acquaintance she can seem awkward and silent. Nevertheless, she is a splendid girl and I can recommend her warmly.

Yours sincerely,

P. F. Woodhurst.

P.F. Woodhurst
(Headmaster)

1 Montyville Road,
Greatcaster,
Wessex

2nd October

Dear Mrs Jenkins,

I would like to apply for the post of clerical asistant at Timkins Products Ltd.

I left school last September and gained'O' levels in English (D), Maths (C), Geography (E), French (D), Physics (C). I also passed RSA Typing and Office Practice.

Apart from my school work I am in the St John's Ambulance Brigade and the Greatcaster branch of Help-the-Aged. I am also a meber of the Local Baptist church where I am a Sunday school teacher.

I have always seen my future career in office work and am confident I could do the job at Timkins Products well.

Yours sincerely,

Karen Walsh

Karen Walsh

THE ROYAL GRAMMAR SCHOOL
PARKS ROAD
GREATCASTER

Headmistress:
V.A. Matlin B.A. Ph.D

7th October

Dear Mrs Jenkins

Thank you for your letter concerning Karen Walsh's application for the post of junior clerical assistant.

Karen was a solid worker and gained a fair range of examination results, taking 'O' levels in English, Maths, History, Geography, French, Biology and Physics. She stayed on an extra year to do typing and office practice and retake some 'O' levels.

She was not one of our highest flyers but she kept at it and eventually gained creditable results. As a character she was pleasant and likeable without being outstanding in any particular way.

She was co-operative and reasonably well liked by both staff and pupils.

Yours sincerely,

V. Matlin

Verna Matlin

---

193 Hastings Road
Bentley
Nr Greatcaster
Wessex

Dear Sir or Madam,

I am interested in the job recently advertised in the Greatcaster Echo. I left school last September with 4 CSEs and one 'O' level and I think I could be successful in the sort of job you discribe

Yours faithfully
William Bartlett
W.S. Bartlett.

St Stimlins School
Greatcaster
Wessex

Headmaster P F Woodhurst B.Ed

Mrs. A. Jenkins,
Personnel Officer,
Timkins Products Ltd.,
Astra House,
Greatcaster

8th October

Dear Mrs. Jenkins,

Thank you for your enquiry concerning William S. Bartlett. William was a pupil at St. Stimlins from the first to the fifth year. In his final examinations he gained CSEs in English (Grade 3), History (Grade 4) and Maths (Grade 1) with an 'O' level (Grade D) in Art.

Both his year tutor and form teacher felt that he could have achieved more than he did at school. He tended to be more interested in his out-of-school activities than in his examination work. He was a keen member of the Computer Club, played for the school's first X1 at football and was a member of the Drama Club, taking part in at least three school productions.

William was popular with his peers, though some members of staff considered him occasionally unreliable. There is no doubt that he is a bright, articulate lad who has the ability to succeed in an occupation that catches his imagination.

I can therefore recommend him for consideration. If I can be of any further assistance, please do not hesitate to get in touch.

Yours sincerely,

P.F. Woodhurst

P.F. Woodhurst
(Headmaster)

13 Cobham Grove
Greatcaster
Wessex

19th October

Dear Mrs Jenkins,

I do apologise for applying so late but I have only just returned home from a short visit. If I am not too late, I would very much like to be considered for the post of Junior Clerical Assistant at Timkins Ltd.

I got 3 'O' levels, Maths (C) English (C) and Art (B) and 4 CSEs Physics (2), French (3), History (4), Geography (4).

If I can surpply any further information please get in touch. My home number is Greatcaster 0704.

Yours in haste,

Silvia Morley

Answers

Information

If some of the activities in this book have helped you to think about your reading and to try out different ways of reading for different purposes, then this is far more important than whether your answers were 'right' or 'wrong'.

Many of the conclusions you have arrived at will probably be different in some details from those of other students. This is as it should be, since it shows that you are an active reader. Your individual experiences and attitudes have helped to bring the text to life.

However, since some of the questions are more factual than others and since you may wish to compare your versions of some passages with their originals, here are some answers.

How close you got to them is not so important to your learning as the route by which you arrived!

1 What's missing?
Lifesaving calm; methods; effective; bank; stretch; out; branch; object; way; throw; something; confidence; time; next; quicker; possible; held; victim; shallow; victim; rowing; swimming; rescuer; above; swim; tow; clothing; impede; out; depth.

Lost in the jungle leg; injured; allow; distance; have; food; last; days; plane; shade; gets; cold; morning; pair; wooden; took; used; from; piece; metal; saw; tired; slept; crutches; quite; smoke; habitation; close; greatly; but; leg; very; have; choice; forest; help; night; prayed; collected; drink; instruments; Indians; meet; walk.

Poem pyramids; piled; tipped; silent; peered; mumble; towering; troubling; shining; sticks; title: The Gamekeeper's Dotage.

Readers' letters

a) I'm learning to drive and will be taking my test in a few weeks' time but I let myself be talked into doing a very stupid thing two nights ago. My parents are away on a two week holiday and have left the car. So my friend persuaded me to take it so we could drive to the disco. Only while I was parking it I scraped all down one side. I'm so scared about what my parents will say when they see it. They keep it in the street so should I say that another car scraped it? Please help.

b) I come from the North and recently I moved down to London with my parents. But I feel really left out and different at school because of my accent. I'm sure everyone makes fun of it behind my back and I hate it. I have even tried talking like the others a bit but it always comes out wrong. What can I do?

c) I got to know two very tough girls who live on an estate near me but I stopped seeing them when I realized how nasty they were. The trouble is when I knew them I gave them my dinner money to buy cigarettes, mainly because I was scared of what they'd do if I didn't. Now whenever they see me they jeer at me and ask for more money. They threaten me too. What can I do?

2 Fitting it together
Passport to peril
e, f, c, a, d, g, b
a) She replied to a request for photographs of the French Channel coast.
b) She was French-born, and presumably knew the country and spoke the language.
c) She pretended to be his wife, and claimed to be leader of the group.
d) i) detailed arrangements to split up the team and send them away
ii) she stayed alive, even though she experienced extreme suffering
iii) extremely unpleasant questioning, often involving torture.
e) It came from a magazine for young people. The main clues which tell you this are:
–the 'catchy' headline title *Passport to Peril.*
–the style of the writing, which is closer to journalism than a textbook, e.g. 'Too late!'
–there is too little factual information for an encyclopaedia entry.
–it could not be part of a book by Churchill, because he would have written about himself as 'I'.

The lesson

b, d, g, j, h, e, a, i, f, c

a) The execution of a criminal.
b) The pupils in the classroom. It is a play on words: it is close to 'hooligan'. (See Roger McGough's other poem '*Nooligan*' in *You Tell Me*, Puffin).
c) Again it is a play on words and meanings. There is a well-known phrase 'First come, first served'. Here the phrase is given a nasty (but funny) twist by inserting one letter 'severed'.

Making cheese straws
d, e, i, b, j, k, c, f, l, a, g, h

The gates
a) Geoffrey Moller, a first-year pupil.
b) Elgan Comprehensive School.
c) He has an 'uncontrollable fear' of school and hates it.
d) He feels dizzy, as if he is in a dream.
e) He gets over the school gates and runs to a bus stop to go home.

b, h, e, d, g, a, f, c

Short story
a) He is planning to commit a murder and disappear.
b) He has been embezzling money.
c) His wife.
d) Unknown to him, his wife has invited friends to their house to celebrate his fortieth birthday. When he arrives with the body of his victim, they are all waiting.

f, b, a, c, e, d, h, g

3 Reasons for reading

The school day
a) West Germany b) Spain c) 3½ hours d) 12.30 e) Portugal

The population explosion
a) About 42 million
b) The death rate
c) Edward Jenner
d) A census is an official count of the inhabitants of a country.
e) Dirt, disease, lack of medical knowledge, poor food and bad living conditions.
f) Trade with overseas countries was increasing. This brought better food into England, and also cotton, which was healthier to wear than wool.
g) No

h) Neither axis of the graph is clearly labelled. The *table* shows the population in 1900 as about 36 million; but the *graph* shows it as about 43 million.

Airline

a) It is the alphabetical order
b) i) 4817 miles
ii) 3044 miles
iii) 3612 miles
c) i) 5842 km
ii) 4899 km
d) Amsterdam
e) Prestwick
f) i) Edmonton
ii) Vancouver

School textbook

a) A History textbook
b) iv) It is an account of the development of trade unions
c) There are several things that identify the passage as part of a history textbook.
For example:
–the use of the past tense, e.g. 'accepted'; 'brought'; 'began to develop'; 'became established'.
–the use of dates, e.g. 1720; 1775; 1800.
–key phrases like 'Industrial Revolution'; 'in the eighteenth century'.
–the factual way events are described.
d) The clothworkers once met there regularly as a trade club.
e) i) Most of the workers felt that they were not in a position to change their fate, and that it was part of the accepted pattern of life that some people were more favoured than others.
ii) Members banded together to protect their standard of living and their way of life.
iii) They would stand a better chance of winning their case against their employers.

4 What's next?

Answer

a) i) 'ceremoniously' means 'very formally, with a sense of ceremony'

ii) 'cybernetics' means 'methods of communication or control through the use of machines'

iii) 'galaxies' means 'vast systems of stars (like the Milky Way)'

b) c) d) All these answers are a matter of opinion. The best thing to do is read the rest of the story printed below.

e) 'Is there a God?'
The mighty voice answered without hesitation, without the click of a single relay. 'Yes, NOW there is a GOD.'
Sudden fear flashed on the face of Dwar Ev. He leaped to grab the switch. A bolt of lightning from the cloudless sky struck him down and fused the switch shut.

Do you read me?

a) i) Fenton likes making jokes.
Evidence: he describes Rodney's badges as 'armour plate'.

ii) He works hard.
Evidence: he arranges a Book Fair for the school.

(Other points you can discover for yourself.)

b) The answer depends on what you think a good teacher should be. On the one hand the fifth years seem to like him and he spends a lot of time talking to Rodney about his report. On the other hand he is very sarcastic with Rodney about his badges.

c) Rodney is intelligent and thoughtful but he finds it very difficult to put his thoughts into words. He seems to use his badges as a way of communicating with people.

d) The writer of the story likes describing people in a funny way.
Evidence: 'horrible Hobbers', 'five live authors, all looking repellently like teachers'.
She is sarcastic.
Evidence: 'The Fifth Year, as befitted the enormous strides that they had made in self-discipline during the summer holidays, were left to find their own way.'
She likes funny comparisons.
Evidence: 'first school children, all squeaking like unoiled roller skates'.

e) Rodney, who thinks Liz is lovely, finds it difficult to speak to her. Eddie Hobson thinks Liz is *his* girlfriend and makes threatening noises if anyone else tries to talk to her.

Monday lunchtime brought Fenton and Rodney together again.

'I fear, we're going to see a lot of each other this term,' Fenton sighed. 'You're sailing perilously close to the wind, King. You don't want a total embargo on your cargo, do you?'

Rodney had been practising a new gesture over the weekend. He raised his left eyebrow.

'ROD AGAINST RACISM I like,' said Fenton. 'ROD AGAINST THE BOMB is morally impeccable. However, NO FLIES ON ROD is another matter. When I told you to take the bloody things off your jacket I didn't mean that you should put them anywhere else. That scrum at break, round the coffee machine, was largely caused by your reading public, King, on its hands and knees, perusing your jeans. What the hell is that on the back of your neck?' Rodney turned round so that Fenton could see the badge on his collar: KING'S HEAD. NO COACHES.

'Exquisite lettering. I said nothing on your back.'

'It's under my hair, unless I look down,' Rodney protested.

'It's under your *back* hair,' Fenton said. 'Edit yourself, King.'

Rodney edited himself drastically, removing KING CAN SERIOUSLY DAMAGE YOUR HEALTH, NO U TURNS, NO S BENDS, NO Y FRONTS and DANGER, CONCEALED EXIT from their carefully chosen sites, leaving only a striking model in severe black type on white, after the fashion of London Transport: WATCH THIS SPACE, which he wore until Wednesday.

WATCH THIS SPACE provoked a gratifying curiosity among his readership. Even Hobbers and his little harem displayed some interest in his frontage. When public response had, he judged, reached its peak, he removed WATCH THIS SPACE and pinned another badge in its place.

'Oh look – a new one,' Anna cried, homing in on it. A moment later she recoiled and walked back to Katy with an affronted expression.

'What does it say?' Katy asked. 'Something disgusting?'

'Read it yourself, if you want to know,' Anna said, sulkily. Katy stood up and approached Rodney's table. Rodney obligingly angled his shoulder the better to display his lapel. Katy leaned toward him, flushed, and backed off. Finally Liz, curious in spite of herself, wandered over.

'What does it say, Rod?'

'You wouldn't want to read it,' Rodney said, and folded his arms over his chest. 'I've got a different one for you.' He was aware of Hobbers, glowering over by the window in an attitude of Neanderthal aggression. 'You can look at it later on.'

'Can't I see it now?'

'Not here.' Rodney looked shocked. 'See you at break – outside the library.' He rose swiftly and went out.

'Well then,' Hobbers demanded, with menaces, 'what did it say? What's his badge of the week or flavour of the month this time, then?'

'I don't know. He wouldn't let me look,' Liz said.

'You keep away from him and his badges,' Hobbers said. 'I don't know what the attraction is, the boring little git.'

'He's funny,' she said.

'Funny?'

'Anyway, attraction's not something you'd know much about, is it?' Liz said, shortly. She joined Katy and Anna on their way to class.

'Did you see what it said?' Katy asked.

'No. What did it say?'

'IF YOU CAN READ THIS YOU ARE TOO CLOSE,' Anna snapped.

Liz smiled. 'Oh.'

'What are you grinning about?'

'I suppose that's why he wouldn't let me read it,' Liz said.

At break she went to find Rodney outside the deserted library. He was there, his lapel vacant, and wearing a tie. On the knot of the tie was a badge.

'It better not be something foul,' Liz warned him.

Rodney mimed affronted innocence. Would I do that? asked his arching eyebrows.

Liz leaned toward him and studied the legend: READ THE SMALL PRINT. 'Is that all?'

'Of course it isn't. *Read* the small print.'

'I can see that. What small print?'

'Round the edge,' said Rodney.

'That?' Liz peered, inches away. 'That squiggle? I thought it was the border.'

'It's not a squiggle. It's small print: very small print.'

'Get away, I can't read that.'

'You can if you come near enough,' Rodney said, and held his breath, praying that he had not taken the onions out of last night's hamburger in vain.

'Is it going to be worth it?'

'It's for *you*.'

'And it's not something filthy?'

'Liz,' Rodney said, solemnly, 'if you don't trust me, you'll never find out what it says, will you?'

She was squinting past his chin now. 'I still can't read it.'

'You'll have to come closer, then, won't you?' and he closed his eyes, saying silently, Oh God, make it work, and when he opened them again she was still there, right under his nose, reading the world's smallest love letter round the edge of his tenth badge. He thought, I wonder what would happen if I kissed her, and wished he could ask, but he had run out of badges.

Examination day

a) It seems to have some sinister purpose. Maybe the parents are worried because the result could lead to Dickie being taken away from them, or harmed in some way.
b) He seems bright, alert and questioning about things.
c) It suggests that the government might control many aspects of the lives of its people. For instance, there is a 'Government newspaper'. In other words, it is a totalitarian regime.
d) Either he doesn't know and is ignorant, or perhaps the story takes place on another planet in another solar system.

Dickie sat at the breakfast table and again saw moisture in his mother's eyes. He didn't connect her tears with the exam until his father suddenly brought the subject to light again.

'Well, Dickie,' he said, with a manly frown. 'You've got an appointment today.'

'I know Dad. I hope–'

'Now, it's nothing to worry about. Thousands of children take this test every day. The Government wants to know how smart you are, Dickie. That's all there is to it.'

'I get good marks in school,' he said hesitantly.

'This is different. This is a–special kind of test. They give you this stuff to drink, you see, and then you go into a room where there's a sort of machine–'

'What stuff to drink?' Dickie said.

'It's nothing. It tastes like peppermint. It's just to make sure you answer the questions truthfully. Not that the Government thinks you won't tell the truth, but this stuff makes *sure*.'

Dickie's face showed puzzlement, and a touch of fright. He looked at his mother, and she composed her face into a misty smile.

'Everything will be all right,' she said.

'Of course it will,' his father agreed. 'You're a good boy, Dickie; you'll make out fine. Then we'll come home and celebrate. All right?'

'Yes, sir,' Dickie said.

They entered the Government Educational Building fifteen minutes before the appointed hour. They crossed the marble floors of the great pillared lobby, passed beneath an archway and entered an automatic lift that brought them to the fourth floor.

There was a young man wearing an insignia-less tunic, seated at a polished desk in front of Room 404. He held a clipboard in his hand, and he checked the list down to the Js and permitted the Jordans to enter.

The room was as cold and official as a courtroom, with long benches flanking metal tables. There were several fathers and sons already there, and a thin-lipped woman with cropped black hair was passing out sheets of paper.

Mr Jordan filled out the form, and returned it to the clerk. Then he told Dickie: 'It won't be long now. When they call your name, you just go through the doorway at that end of the room.' He indicated the portal with his finger.

A concealed loudspeaker crackled and called off the first name. Dickie saw a boy leave his father's side reluctantly and walk slowly towards the door.

At five minutes to eleven, they called the name of Jordan.

'Good luck, son,' his father said, without looking at him. 'I'll call for you when the test is over.'

Dickie walked to the door and turned the knob. The room inside was dim, and he could barely make out the features of the grey-tunicked attendant who greeted him.

'Sit down,' the man said softly. He indicated a high stool beside his desk. 'Your name's Richard Jordan?'

'Yes, sir.'

'Your classification number is 600- 115. Drink this, Richard.'

He lifted a plastic cup from the desk and handed it to the boy. The liquid inside had the consistency of buttermilk, tasted only vaguely of the promised peppermint. Dickie downed it, and handed the man the empty cup.

He sat in silence, feeling drowsy, while the man wrote busily on a sheet of paper. Then the attendant looked at his watch, and rose to stand only inches from Dickie's face. He unclipped a penlike object from the pocket of his tunic, and flashed a tiny light into the boy's eyes.

'All right,' he said. 'Come with me, Richard.'

He led Dickie to the end of the room, where a single wooden armchair faced a multi-dialled computing machine. There was a microphone on the left arm of the chair, and when the boy sat down, he found its pinpoint head conveniently at his mouth.

'Now just relax, Richard. You'll be asked some questions, and you think them over carefully. Then give your answers into the microphone. The machine will take care of the rest.'

'Yes, sir.'

'I'll leave you alone now. Whenever you want to start, just say "ready" into the microphone.'

'Yes, sir.'

The man squeezed his shoulder, and left.

Dickie said, 'Ready.'

Lights appeared on the machine, and a mechanism whirred. A voice said: 'Complete this sequence. One, four, seven, ten . . .'

Mr and Mrs Jordan were in the living room, not speaking, not even speculating.

It was almost four o'clock when the telephone rang. The woman tried to reach it first, but her husband was quicker.

'Mr Jordan?'

The voice was clipped; a brisk, official voice.

'Yes, speaking.'

This is the Government Educational Service. Your son, Richard M. Jordan, Classification 600-115, has completed the Government examination. We regret to inform you that his intelligence quotient is above the Government regulation, according to Rule 84, Section 5, of the New Code.'

Across the room, the woman cried out, knowing nothing except the emotion she read on her husband's face.

'You may specify by telephone,' the voice droned on, 'whether you wish his body interred by the Government, or would you prefer a private burial place? The fee for Government burial is ten dollars.'

A lot to learn

a) It makes whatever you ask for or say a reality.
b) He has no container to hold the liquid in, and the machine doesn't provide one. It doesn't share the human understanding that a 'martini' comes in a glass.
c) It suggests perhaps that the 'benefits' of such a machine may still be a problem to humanity and cause as many problems as they might solve.

Ned enlarged the Receiver and prepared for his greatest experiment. He switched on the Materializer, took a deep breath and said, 'Girl.'

The whirring sound swelled and faded. In the Receiver stood a lovely girl. She was naked. Ned had not asked for clothing.

She had freckles, a brace and pigtails. She was eight years old.

'Hell!' said Quinn.

Whirr.

The fireman found two charred skeletons in the smouldering rubble.

5 Keeping alert

Lightning

TRUE: d, f (unless you are in the middle of dense woods), i.
PARTLY TRUE: c, e.
FALSE: a, b, g, h, j.

a) i) 'jettison' means 'discard' or 'throw away'.
ii) 'virtually assured' means 'almost certain'.

iii) 'low profile' means 'no higher than surrounding buildings or trees'.
iv) 'scree slope' means 'a slope of loose slate and stones'.

The blitz

There is no 'right' answer here, but f, d, b and e should be near the top of your list, while i, g and j should be nearer the bottom.

a) i) 'invariably' means 'nearly always'.
ii) 'comprehensible' means 'understandable'.
iii) 'fortifying themselves' probably means 'having a drink and/or something to eat'.
iv) 'indelible picture' means 'unforgettable image or memory'.

A visit to Jamaica

TRUE: a, d, e
FALSE: b, c, f, g, h

a) In some ways Jamaican people were very strict in the ways they expected young people to behave,
e.g.–They had to wear smart school uniform.
–Marcia gets told off for wearing make-up.
–They have strong religious attitudes and the church plays an important part in their lives.
In other ways they seemed very easy-going
e.g.–Young people of both sexes bathed together naked.
–Young people stayed out very late at night.
–Getting pregnant was not looked upon so seriously.

Holiday insurance

a) It simply gives information. No name and address of any insurance company is given.
b) i) loss of luggage or clothing
ii) cancellation of holiday, due to illness for example
iii) delay of holiday due to industrial action
iv) medical expenses, should you be ill or injured
v) an accident causing death or injury
vi) your liability if you cause damage, or injury to others
c) About £8 per adult for a fortnight's cover.
d) You must report the loss to the police within 24 hours and obtain proof that you have done so. One snag might be that you would have to report the loss in person to ensure written proof of notification. A phone call, for instance, would not be enough.
e) The usual cover is £300–£600.
f) i) 'proof of notification' means 'written evidence that you reported the loss'

ii) 'usual cover' means 'the amount the insurance company will normally pay in the event of a claim'
iii) 'holiday curtailment' means 'having your holiday cut short for any reason'
iv) 'personal liability' means 'the compensation or damages you might have to pay if you injured someone or damaged property'

g) £2,000–£2,500.
h) It doesn't list any companies which provide this kind of insurance. Also it doesn't give exact costs, or an idea of costs for holidays outside of Europe.

Keeping fit–past and present

a) i) It benefits both the mind and the body.
ii) Anyone can do it.
iii) It is good for the circulation (heart and lungs) and the limbs (muscles).

b) i) The first writer suggests that the best times are
–morning and evening in the summer
–after breakfast, or from ten to one, in winter.
He also suggests that it is best to walk after meals.
ii) The second writer suggests that it is best to jog when it suits you, but *not* after meals.

c) The first writer seems to be assuming that walks will be taken in the countryside; the second takes account of the fact that many joggers will live in towns.
d) Both stress starting off steadily, within your capability.
e) The first writer recommends walking with a friend *only* if the companion is good company and walks at a similar pace. The second writer recommends jogging with a friend to pass the time.
f) Both writers recommend thick soles, and shoes which are large enough –if necessary–to be worn with thick socks.
g) He has to include a warning about the dangers of traffic and diesel fumes.
h) i) flat
ii) effectively
iii) sit
iv) small room.

6 Think again

An unlikely story

a) The author's title was 'The Spread of Ian Nicol'. The least effective titles are probably 'Ian's Unusual Illness' and 'A Rivetting Tale'. However, you might want to argue differently.
b) A bald patch on the back of his head.
c) The patch begins to look like a face. Ian has stabbing pains, and he eats 'enough for two men'.
d) There is some evidence in the story that each of these is true. It is a matter of interpretation whether you feel the balance to lie with lack of sympathy or reassuring matter-of-factness. (The same is probably true of real visits to the doctor or the hospital!)
e) It looks as though the cycle is about to start again.

Acknowledgements

The author and publisher are grateful to the following copyright holders for permission to reproduce material:

page 18: 'Passport to Peril', *Look and Learn*, 18 July 1981
page 20: 'The Lesson' from *In the Glassroom* by Roger McGough, Jonathan Cape Ltd
page 27: table from *Europe at School*, Norman Newcombe, Methuen and Co. Ltd
page 28: extract from *Britain Since 1700* by R. J. Cootes, Longman
page 43: extract from *Schools OK* by Jan Mark, Evans Brothers Ltd
page 51: extract from *Survival for Young People* by Anthony Greenbank, Harrap
page 56: 'Trip to Jam Down' from *Our Lives* by Marcia Chevers, The English Centre, London SW1
page 62: *The Gentle Jog to fitness*, Health Education Council, London
page 71: 'The Spread of Ian Nicol' from *Unlikely Stories Mostly* by Alasdair Gray, Canongate Publishing Ltd

The publishers have made every attempt to clear permission with all copyright holders but would be glad to hear from any unacknowledged copyright holders.